# MALTA
## 'My Island'

# MALTA
## 'My Island'

### Malta – Il Gzira Tieghi

## Mark Harland

New Edition Published by MVH Publishing 2020

A CIP catalogue record for this book is available from the British Library.

ISBN 978-0-9935895-3-9 (Paperback)

Book layout and cover design by Clare Brayshaw

Back cover: The Chalet Ghar Id Dudd in Sliema depicted in its heyday in the 1930's and the State flag of Queensland which has depicted a Maltese Cross since 1901. Does anybody know why?

Prepared and printed by:

York Publishing Services Ltd
64 Hallfield Road
Layerthorpe
York
YO31 7ZQ

Tel: 01904 431213

Website: www.yps-publishing.co.uk

# FOREWORD

I have been tempted to write this book for some time. Writing a memoir, which I do from time to time, is a very different kettle of fish to writing novels. In 2007 I wrote *Your Country Needs You*, a novel set in England, which readers probably assumed was my home country. They assumed wrongly. I was born in Malta, that tiny speck of Miocene limestone slap bang in the middle of the Mediterranean Sea. I am immensely proud that the island which was awarded the George Cross for bravery in 1942 was also the island that gave me my birth and infant nurture in 1953.

Two things I definitely inherited from my maternal grandfather were a fondness for gardening and a powerful and retentive memory. The latter holds me in good stead for writing this book. I suppose you could call it a memoir, but it is also a story of my relationship with Malta and its people. It is a story that is not yet complete.

I should like to thank Tony Ellul for his assistance when I was stuck for the spelling and meaning of many Maltese names. Grazzii hafna, my friend.

**Mark Harland**

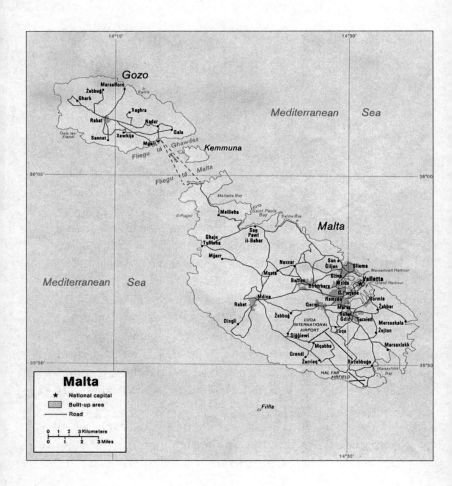

# 1.

For centuries if not millennia the island of Malta, or, to be geographically correct, the Maltese Archipelago, has been the centre of political and military attention. Most European and Middle Eastern powers have wanted to possess it.

A few years ago I was very taken with Sir Trevor McDonald's *Secret Mediterranean* TV series in which he interviewed Joe Said, who was then Malta's Director of Tourism, who said: 'We have seen them all. The Arabs, the Greeks, the Carthaginians, the Romans, the Phoenicians, the French and last of all the British. We have taken the best they had to offer and adopted them as our own.'

Powerful words, indeed, and so true. I, and hundreds of other 'Brits' were born there because Britain was the last colonial power to possess Malta, if indeed one nation can ever own another. Back in 1953 Britain was still a major world power, albeit less powerful than before a second World War had shed it of many of its overseas territories and all its money and foreign exchange. The political humiliation of the Suez fiasco was yet to come and the legacy of the War was a large Naval Fleet based in Malta with substantial air and land forces to protect it.

So, like many other sons and daughters of naval, military and associated British Government personnel, I was born at the David Bruce Naval Hospital in M'Tarfa. This tiny township on the other side of the valley from Mdina, the ancient and former capital of Malta, now has its name stamped into the passports as the place of birth of many a Brit. I wonder though how many have gone back to take a peek at this truly historic building? I did, but more of that later.

I have the vaguest memory of running around under some palm trees when I was about two years old. Years later, five years in fact, my mother pointed them out to me. The area was known locally as simply The Palms and they were on the site now occupied by the huge hotel near the saltpans at Salina Bay. We lived in Spinola Road adjacent to Paceville, which today is the scene of Malta's busiest night life. We kept chickens for fresh eggs and when they stopped laying they went into the pot as my father indelicately expressed it.

On the hot summer evening that I came into this world Dad drank beer in Dick's Bar, and apparently telephoned the hospital every hour to see if I had arrived. Telephones were rare in those days so Dad probably used the location as an excuse. Not that an ex-matelot needed one of course.

Almost nobody had a car in those days and it was a long bus ride the next day to see my mother and his son and heir. By the time my sister Linda arrived eighteen months later Dad had bought a brand new Triumph Mayflower. Most of 'The Boys', as Dad called his colleagues, purchased new cars to take back to the UK at the end of their three year tours of duty and if they kept them for two years they were tax free.

Dad worked as a radio supervisor at a RNWT (Royal Naval Wireless Telegraphy) station, known simply as Dingli, which was quite inaccessible unless you had transport. A works bus took most of The Boys to work. Dingli was the highest point of the island and the cluster of radio masts and antennae had the best chance of picking up foreign (mostly Soviet) military communications. It would prove its worth during the Cuban Missile Crisis in 1962, but that's another story.

With the Mayflower ordered from Mizzi's garage in Sliema, Dad took driving lessons from his colleagues Maurice Waines and Jimmy Stewart. In those days the local Sergeant from Rabat police station was the official examiner and Dad duly took time out from his shift to take the test.

He failed.

'How much did you give him for the church, Vic?' enquired Jimmy in his Gateshead twang.

Dad was dumbfounded.

'What do you mean?'

'The Boys always give him something for the local church – don't tell me nobody told you. Half a crown always goes down well.'

A few weeks later and Dad retook the test. He passed. Family legend has it that he gave the Sergeant ten bob to make absolutely sure.

I don't recall it but my mother's parents visited us in 1953 as they were anxious to see their new grandson. There were no scheduled flights in those days so they travelled by train to Messina in southern Italy, thence to Syracuse in Sicily and finally took a passage on a tiny ship called the MV *Star of Malta*. The whole journey would have taken no less than four days.

The *Star of Malta* had a rich history; it was originally built in 1925 for a wealthy Cincinnati businessman called Julius Fleischmann. Many emigrant Germans had found the rolling countryside surrounding the Ohio River symptomatic of their native Rhineland and had settled there in their thousands. Fleischmann was President of Fleischmann Yeast and brewing was Cincinnati's main industry as you might expect with its Germanic population. Julius became fabulously rich and had the ship built as a luxury yacht. It bore a striking resemblance to the famous *Christina O* of Onassis fame and if it were painted white with a buff funnel few would spot the difference. I wonder if my grandparents knew they were travelling in a millionaire's plaything? Probably not. Isn't Google wonderful?

Granny particularly was a great traveller and adventurer. They owned a successful hotel in Scarborough, the Marina, before the War and one day she announced that she was going to Switzerland to hire a Swiss chef. Travelling alone she took a coach to Basel, interviewed several candidates, chose one and promptly headed back with him a few days later. Poor Grandad, on the other hand, was probably more worried about the fate of his chrysanthemums back home. It was probably an ordeal for him but Granny would have enjoyed every second. They would visit Malta again in 1961 as I will detail later.

In the autumn of 1955 with Dad's tour of duty at an end we left Malta. The Triumph Mayflower was shipped to Liverpool and we, now a family of four, flew back to Gatwick on a Vickers Viking aircraft. Apparently I behaved absolutely disgracefully all the way. So ended my first spell in Malta.

# 2.

After five years' living in Scarborough I was by now seven years old. Our small but nice house was near Peasholm Park and was named Delimara after a small village in Malta where Dad used to go swimming. At five I attended Lisvane School for boys, a little up-market public school that was the normal entry point for Scarborough College, an expensive fee paying boarding school that also took day boys from the town and surrounding areas.

I did well. My teacher, Miss Shaw, took a shine to me and when, in 1960, my father wrote to the school to inform them that we were being posted back to Malta she was very sorry to see me go. On my last day there in July 1960 she presented me with a Bible and had written inside *For very good work at Scarborough Pre-Preparatory School. Miss Shaw.* I wept buckets. Needless to say I still have the Bible.

Granny and Grandad were sorry that we were going abroad again but no doubt Granny was already planning her next trip which next time would be by air. How exciting! In any case the *Star of Malta* was by then out of service having been badly damaged following a grounding off Dragonara Point where the casino is today. Grandad asked me one day how long we would be away. My reply passed into family folklore.

'I don't know Grandad but I'll be ten when we get back.'

Dad flew to Malta on his own at the end of July. Mum, Linda and myself didn't leave until mid-August. On our last day in the house we sat on the stairs and ate a pork pie washed down with a flask of tea. The furniture had gone into store and all we had left were a few clothes and our suitcases which were at Granny's where we were staying for a few days prior to flying out ourselves. The great day arrived and we said our goodbyes to tearful grandparents who promised to come and see us. They did, too.

We travelled by train first to York and then to King's Cross via Peterborough. A very kind man who was in our compartment worked for Cadbury's and gave us a huge bar of milk chocolate. It didn't last long between the three of us. We were met in London by Dad's eldest brother John and sister Eva who came with us to Victoria Station where we boarded the train for Gatwick. Uncle John also said he would do his best to come and visit us in Malta. It proved to be another promise kept and I will write later about that. It was almost dark by the time the four engined Vickers Viscount took off. Next stop was Nice in the south of France for refuelling. The plane probably carried about fifty passengers. Today as I fly from Manchester to Malta in a twin-jet Airbus A320 that carries a hundred-and-fifty passengers non-stop it makes me realise just how primitive aviation was in those days.

I was far too excited to sleep. A violent thunder and lightning storm descended on us just before we landed in Nice. It put paid to any ideas of getting off the plane and we were delayed quite a while. It was probably too dangerous to deploy the fuel bowser during the storm. After more than an hour on the ground we took off again and headed southeast out into the Mediterranean. I was going home!

It started to get light and I sat next to a window on the port side and watched the sun come up. A few hours later and Malta came into view: it looked like a floating rock, which, when you think about it, is exactly what it is [the pedant will say, no it isn't, it's the top of a mountain range the rest of which is under water]. It looked hot even from the air. The plane landed and we walked down the steps onto the tarmac. I could see my Dad and Maurice Waines (Uncle Moss to me) waving from the public viewing gallery.

It seemed no time at all before all five of us were in Maurice's two tone Wolseley saloon. It was a tight squeeze with one suitcase on the back seat with Mum and Linda. I was in the front on the red leather bench seat with Dad and I couldn't help but notice how brown his legs were in contrast to his white shorts. He had been in the sun for only a month but already looked like a native. I remember that both my Dad and Maurice smoked cigarettes all the way to our destination, St. Paul's Bay. It was still only about seven in the morning but already it was hot, probably about thirty degrees Celsius although it was all Fahrenheit in those days so I'm guessing about eighty-five in old money.

There was almost no traffic to be seen apart from the odd horse and cart although it was still early of course. We had a mild panic on the way when a wasp flew in through the open window and tried to take up residence in Dad's shorts. Maurice pulled the car up smartly and Dad ejected himself faster than Martin-Baker's finest to release the culprit from his Bombay Bloomers. The air was blue but another Senior Service later and all was well with the world again. We arrived at Dolphin Flats to be met by Maurice's wife Joyce who laid on tea and bacon sandwiches for us all. I also had my first ever taste of 7 Up, the fizzy drink described by the bottlers as *a kiss of lemon and a kiss of lime.* Joyce and Maurice lived on the second floor and our new home was to be on the ground floor, which was much bigger at twice the size. It was surrounded by high walls and proved to be blisteringly hot with the sun reflecting like a laser off the whitewashed walls. When the occupants of the flat immediately above moved we would move up one storey but that's a story I'll tell you later.

Lots of our stuff had already arrived from Scarborough and in between shifts Dad had unpacked most of our possessions. In those days most flats in Malta were ready furnished and equipped with all manner of household items right down to things like corkscrews and cutlery. Even ashtrays. With my dad, not to mention Maurice, we sure needed them. Dolphin Flats were sited on a hill called XemXija (pronounced shemshia) and the view over the bay towards the village of St. Paul's Bay itself was superb. The water looked blue and inviting although at that point I still couldn't swim. There would be plenty of time to learn.

I didn't wear a shirt for the whole of the first day. Big mistake. I got huge water blisters on each shoulder like poached eggs. Mum laughed as she pricked them with a pin and watery goo ran down my back from each one. I wore a T-shirt for the next few days although my legs and arms got sunburnt and I was introduced to the charms of calamine lotion that was dabbed onto the affected areas with cotton wool. It hardened off and left pink bomb-sites all over your arms and legs. It was dreadful stuff.

'That will teach you to be careful of the sun out here,' was an oft repeated mantra from both parents.

Being born in the Maltese summer didn't immunise you against the heat, I was sorry to discover. Nor did it provide any protection against the squadrons of mosquitoes that attacked my white flesh every evening after dark. Bottles of

TCP and calamine were consumed at almost the same rate as bottles of Hop Leaf, the local beer that Dad and Maurice cooled down with at almost every opportunity. We had a fan in our bedrooms and I soon discovered that if you ran it at maximum power then such was the blast that mosquitoes couldn't fly through it. The downside was that the noise of the fan kept you awake.

There was a scream one night from Linda's bedroom. She had spotted a gecko, a small lizard, on her bedroom ceiling. No amount of explanation to her that the gecko would eat all the mosquitoes did any good. She was mortified. The problem was caused by quite a lot of standing water in the area and there was little if any spraying of insecticide done by the local council.

We bought loads of spray called Shelltox from the stores in the village and we were also introduced to something called Moon Tiger. This was amazing yet so simple. It worked like a slow burning firework and resembled a coiled up snake about six inches across. It was dark green and had the texture of sealing wax. You took it out of its paper wrapper and balanced it on a small metal plinth made of tin with a sharp point which stuck into the centre of the coil. The thing was thus about two inches off the base and you placed it on a plate or dish. Then you lit the end like lighting a Catherine wheel except instead of spinning round it burnt slowly, giving off fumes which were not unpleasant to humans but were deadly to mosquitoes. I suppose it was a bit like a circular joss stick. The room quickly filled with these fumes and protected you all night. In the morning, on the plate, was a perfect coil of ash that resembled that from a cigarette. These coils worked and were very inexpensive.

Dad announced one morning that his new car was ready to collect from Mizzi's in Sliema, the same company he had bought the Mayflower from five years earlier. Uncle Moss took Dad into town to collect it. I went along for the ride as school had not yet started after the summer holidays. I sat in the back which quickly filled up with smoke from the Senior Service and Piccadilly cigarettes. I coughed a lot despite all the windows being open. In those days air-conditioning in cars probably wasn't even in the mind's eye of the designers let alone the manufacturers. Mizzi's was on a corner right at the top of Savoy Road and as we pulled onto the forecourt I remember Dad shouting *There she is* as he pointed to a grey Morris Oxford with shiny new plates on it. The paperwork completed, Dad got into the driver's seat and I jumped into the front alongside him. Well, almost. Uncle Moss grabbed me by the collar and hauled me out.'Your dad hasn't driven for a long time so you're coming with me, Marcus.'

He and his wife Joyce were the only people in the world, to this day, who ever called me that. That was fine by me as they were surrogate Godparents, both of them having been at my Christening in Holy Trinity Church in Rudolf Street, Sliema, in 1953.

We set off back to St. Paul's Bay with Uncle Moss and myself following Dad with a margin of about a hundred yards which Moss lengthened to two hundred yards once we were nicely out onto the Coast Road. Very wise. Dad's driving was just appalling and Moss could not stop laughing as Dad veered from one side of the road to another, albeit on a particularly winding stretch of the road. He had a near miss with the St. Paul's Bay bus coming in the other direction as we passed, as sod's law would have it, on a nasty bend near where the Splash & Fun Park is today. The bus driver sounded his horn for ages but I doubt it would have registered with Dad. We didn't stop on the journey of about half-an-hour and I just assumed that he went all that time without a fag. Moss, on the other hand, was well practised in the art of removing a fag from the packet in his shirt pocket with his left hand and then holding the box of matches and the wheel in his left while striking the match with his right. The extinguished match was then ejected from the car via the little triangular quarter-light that they don't make on cars any more. Just as well Dad didn't try that – at least not until he'd got used to driving again.

We hadn't owned a family car since 1958 when Dad sold the Mayflower for more money than he had paid for it having kept it for the statutory two years to avoid what was then called purchase tax. Our house in Scarborough was sited only two hundred yards from a theatre called the Floral Hall. Dad had stuck a home made 'Please do not park here' sign outside our gate which was remarkably well respected. One day in July 1958 there was a knock at the door and a smiling and polite gentleman enquired if he could park outside every day for two hours around midday as he was performing for the summer at the Floral Hall and had nowhere to park during rehearsals.

It was none other than Benny Hill!

Dad told Benny that actually he no longer owned a car and that he was welcome to park there any time. In return Benny promised to entertain my sister and me in the garden if we were there when he parked up. He kept his word and would pull funny faces for us through the lattice fence for many minutes before walking briskly uphill the two hundred yards to the theatre. How many people can genuinely boast that they were privately entertained by Benny, in my book the best comedian this country ever produced? Today he would be pilloried by all the miserable, feminist, politically correct and humourless tossers that seemingly permeate every level of British society. I'd hang 'em all if I could.

# 3.

After two weeks it was time to go to school. I was dreading it.

Dad took Linda and me to school for our first day there. We went in the Morris Oxford which fortunately Dad had mastered by then. It was a good half-hour's bus ride from where we lived, probably about five miles as the crow flies but much longer via the coast road that weaved and meandered first through the narrow roads of St. Paul's Bay itself then on the twisting snake of tarmac that more or less followed the rocky coastline southeastwards towards the St. Andrew's area. Today the area is known locally as Pembroke and is the site of a park and ride facility.

When we got to the school we arrived at the same time as two other fathers taking their sons for their first day too. Dad knew them both as they were work colleagues: Jack Church and his son Michael and Bob Davis and his son Michael! Fortunately they were known as Mick and Mike respectively which avoided confusion. All three of us were going to be in the same class, 1A. My new school, to give it its full title St. Andrew's Army Primary School, was actually very pleasant.

Previously I had only ever had one teacher, the lovely Miss Shaw, and I hoped my new mistress was going to be as nice. It turned out that 'she' was a man called Mr Hendy. I was horrified, but I need not have worried as Mr Hendy was a nice man. It took a little while getting used to having girls as classmates as Lisvane School had been all boys. I took a shine to a girl called Penelope, an Army officer's daughter who spoke most politely even at seven. Years later while watching episodes of *Thunderbirds* and Lady Penelope I often wondered what had happened to my little friend who I hoped had turned out to be as posh as the TV character. Penelope was brilliant at painting, particularly fish, I recall.

I settled in easily and found myself miles ahead in arithmetic and English, although my spelling left as much to be desired then as it does now. One of the first essays we had to write was *What we did at the weekend* so I pretended that we had collected Dad's new car that weekend instead of mid-week. I retold the tale of Dad's poor driving and the near miss with the bus. Mr Hendy corrected any errors with a red Army pen and I remember he changed *Uncle Morris* to *Uncle Maurice*. Clearly Morris Oxfords were cars and not Uncles. I never made the mistake again.

On the second and for every day thereafter Linda and I went to school on the bus provided by the Army, a khaki coloured Bedford that made the most unholy noises in first and second gears. Its first pick-up point was at the top of XemXija Hill near our flats and I quickly made friends with another classmate called Vaughan Gordon. He was slim with blond, almost white, hair and spoke with an almost unintelligible accent which took me weeks to get used to. His father was a Royal Marines Sergeant and the family came from Lynemouth in Northumberland. As the Gordons lived in a block of flats less than a hundred yards away Vaughan and I spent a lot of time together at weekends. It was my first experience of the Geordie habit of putting the word 'man' at the end of almost every sentence. Do ya wanna go fishing man? Do ya wanna a 7 Up man? I found it most odd. Still do.

Dad bought me my first ever fishing rod from the ironmongers in the village of Bur-Marrad about two miles southeast of St. Paul's Bay on the road to the town of Mosta. It was a one street village with a selection of shops including a dressmaker which was very popular with Mum and 'Aunty' Joyce. I seem to remember a new dress cost ten shillings. A Maltese pound ranked pari-pasu with Sterling at the time so I guess that was cheap. The shop was probably the Prada of its day.

Maltese fishing rods consisted of two or more straight sections of bamboo slotted together a bit like a chimney sweep's pole. Mine was four sections long and when assembled was a good twenty feet long or a good four times my own height. Vaughan, who had been in Malta a few months longer than me, was by now an old hand and showed me the ropes. We cut lengths of fishing line almost as long as the rod and tied one end into the metal loop that was permanently fixed to the end of the top section. At the other end a large sewing needle was affixed and skewered through a wine cork which was the float. A suitable hook was selected and tied on tight. For bait we used bread paste made by simply mixing a slice of white bread with water until it turned into a sort of dough.

We walked up the hill, and down a path to the rocky sea edge. With the hook through a lump of dough about the size of a walnut I cast seawards. The dough parted from the hook mid flight. I had put too heavy a chunk of bait on the hook so repeated the exercise with a much smaller piece. We waited and waited and waited. Eventually the cork started to bob around and then suddenly it plunged under the surface.

'Strike man!' yelled Vaughan. I hadn't a clue what he meant. Eventually I got what he meant and I heaved up on the quite heavy rod expecting something at least as big as a salmon or a cod which I had seen back in England.

The silver fish was about two and a half inches long. I couldn't believe it. I lowered it onto the rocks and it was still jumping about on the hook. Would you believe it actually threw itself off the hook back into the sea. So ended my fishing adventure.

Summer slowly started to turn to autumn and the mosquitoes that hadn't been Moon Tigered or Shelltoxed took a breather from attacking us. It actually started to feel quite cool at night. Next door to the Waines on the fourth floor lived Squadron Leader Hennessy, his wife and daughter Kim who was a classmate of Linda's. They had a new Morris Mini which hadn't long been around. The front windows slid backwards and forwards and the door handle was a piece of wire which you tugged on to open it – unbelievable now, looking back, but who would have thought then in 1960 that the Mini would become an icon of Britishness and a major commercial success?

The Squadron Leader was an Avro Shackleton pilot based at Ta'Qali Aerodrome near Mosta. 'The Shack' was a maritime patrol aircraft, sometimes described as ten thousand rivets flying in close formation. It was actually derived from the Lancaster bomber and adapted for long range over water patrols with extra fuel tanks and cameras. Fifty-five years later it is embarrassing to admit that Britain today doesn't possess even one single plane capable of maritime reconnaissance. It is yet another example of how a Europe obsessed, sea blind bunch of goons who claim to govern us have in reality forgotten we are still a maritime nation. I could go on but I won't.

Our man Hennessy used to fly regularly to RAF Akrotiri in Cyprus and return with baskets full of juicy Jaffa oranges which he handed round to all of us. They were a nice alternative to the native Maltese oranges which were a tad on the bitter side and used for jams, marmalade and a local drink called Kinnie which I will mention again later. There was just one downside to the Hennessy family. They had a pet black cat which for some reason had a penchant for jumping through even small gaps in an open bedroom window, leaping onto the nearest bed whether occupied by a human or not and then curling up and going to sleep.

After it scared the daylights out of my sister in the middle of one particular night Dad decided that it was time for pussy cat to emigrate. Just before going on a night-shift one evening he tempted pussy into the flat with a bit of fish and then into a cardboard box. He left it at a farmhouse just outside Dingli where as far as he knew it lived a long and happy life with other cats and probably a heap of fresh pigeons to prey on.

Every day for about a week Mrs Hennessy could be heard knocking at doors enquiring, 'Has anybody seen my pussy?' Linda was never told lest she accidentally spilled the beans to Kim. That's life. Linda has always been fond of cats and would definitely not have approved of Dad's actions.

Soon afterwards the Hennessys were posted back to the UK anyway so they were spared the costs of quarantine which were enormous in those days. Every repatriated dog or cat had to spend six months in a Ministry detention centre to demonstrate it was free of rabies. There was none of this Pet Passport lark in those days.

They weren't the only ones to move out. The Noonan family who lived directly above us decided to move into Sliema and Dad arranged with the landlords for us to move up a floor. We were all pleased as it gave us the chance to escape the heat of the ground floor. Upstairs also had a better view of the Bay and the sea not to mention a cooling breeze off the latter, particularly at night. The move itself was very memorable and was to be accomplished in one day. I don't know how many Hop Leafs Dad and Uncle Moss consumed before they came up with this plan.

Dolphin Flats were built into a solid rock hill. Its layout was unusual in that access to the ground floor flat was via a long concrete drive that came up from the seaside road. Vehicular access to all the flats above was via XemXija Hill, a four hundred yards trip. Thus moving just one storey up was going to be a protracted affair with furniture and possessions having to be loaded onto a truck, driven four hundred yards and then unloaded. To make matters even worse the first storey, to where we were moving, was accessed by a flight of some twenty stone steps down from the small car park where the truck, if used, would have to be unloaded. To avoid this back breaking and laborious nightmare Dad and Moss came up with a plan that involved winching everything from the ground floor by rope up to the balcony of our new flat. The balcony in question was huge and almost circumnavigated the whole flat. Large, double folding doors led from the lounge to the balcony and were wide enough to accommodate the biggest pieces of furniture. In theory, anyway.

The great day arrived and it was probably a Saturday as I was not at school. We have all seen those programmes on TV where a bunch of Scouts or Army cadets take part in initiative tests where they have to transfer, say, a heavy crate, across a river or ditch using only three wooden stakes, a length of rope that Albert Pierrepoint would have turned his nose up at and a box of matches. Dad and Moss started with fairly light items like rattan balcony furniture. They were secured to one end of one of the several lengths of rope that Dad had purloined from somewhere and easily hauled up one at a time and temporarily stacked on the capacious balcony.

So far so good. The flats being furnished, there was no requirement to send up heavy furniture such as armchairs. There was tons of other stuff, though, including several large and heavy suitcases and trunks full of clothes and bedding. One particular case was just too heavy and although the rope held, the handle to which it was affixed did not, and just a foot or so from grabbing distance it parted from the case itself and crashed fifteen feet onto the concrete below. Surprisingly, although the case was dented it did not split open: they were proper cases in those days with brass corners. I think it was brought round by car later.

There was one particular piece of wicker furniture that Mum wanted in the lounge and not on the balcony. Sod's law prevailed: it was just a few inches too long to go through even the double doors. However its dimensions could be reduced by removing it from its wrought iron base and legs. Enter a spanner and Allen keys and it was soon dismembered and then reassembled inside the lounge. It was, as they say, a long day but we all slept soundly in our new home.

Christmas was coming and if Malta had geese then they would have been getting fat. Christmas cards arrived from uncles, aunts and grandparents and in those days you really did feel a million miles away. Linda and I received postal orders as gifts which Dad cashed at the NAAFI Post Office for us and changed into Maltese money, usually ten shillings in value. I was saving up for an electric train-set and all the money went into a piggy bank (there was no need to worry about offending Muslims in those days. There weren't any! Well, not unless you flew two hundred miles west to Tunisia).

Cards and presents were posted well in advance with care taken not to miss the last date for surface mail as it was called in those days. The last date was probably about 1st December to allow for the transit time from Malta to Southampton (probably via Gibraltar) and then sorting and onward delivery within the UK. Air Mail, for parcels at least, was prohibitively expensive so we were very surprised indeed just a few days before Christmas to receive a note from the postman to say we had to collect an Air Mail parcel from Mosta Post Office. The postman explained that duty had to be paid on it first before it could be handed over.

We were all intrigued by this and Dad said he had never known anything like it in Malta before. So late one afternoon when the shadows were long and darkness was approaching I went with Dad in the car to Mosta, a twenty minute drive. In those days the GPO was almost opposite the huge church that dominates the Mosta skyline. We parked almost outside and walked in. Dad gave the clerk the docket the postman had given him and we didn't have long to wait. It was a large circular tin like a biscuit tin and well wrapped in several layers of thick brown paper with blobs of red sealing wax dotted all over it as though it had measles or scarlet fever. Several high denomination English postage stamps, all depicting the Queen, of course, dominated the upper side of the wrapping.

'One shilling tax to pay please, Sir,' said the clerk. Dad gulped.

'A shilling? It can hardly be the Crown Jewels can it?'

Reluctantly he paid up. I wanted him to open it in the car but a message written on the outside said *Not to be opened till Christmas Day and a Merry Christmas to you all.* It was to be several days before we discovered the nature of the contents and the identity of the sender.

I think we had a small frozen turkey on Christmas Day with all the usual trimmings. Christmas in Christian Malta was delightful, like England but warmer and sunny too. Lots of visitors popped in for a glass of sherry and a mince pie. Maurice and Joyce and their very young daughter Susan joined in and everybody in the block probably went into everyone else's flat at some time during the day. There was no Queen's Christmas Speech for us because there were no televisions. Father Christmas was very kind to me indeed. A train-set arrived in the form of a black locomotive and six different goods wagons all complete with about twenty feet of track and a battery operated control. I was in my element. York, Peterborough and King's Cross here we come.

After lunch and too much Christmas pudding Dad came into the lounge bearing the parcel we had collected from Mosta.

'Now, let's see what this is shall we?' He had a glint in his eye and sported half a grin. Did he know already?

It weighed a ton. A small knife was produced and the lumps of red sealing wax were prised off the outer layers of thick brown paper. Layer by layer, almost like a game of 'pass the parcel' the paper fell to the floor. We all gasped to see the contents: a huge tin of Quality Street chocolates. On the lid was a short note saying *A merry Christmas from Uncle Frank and Aunty Mary.*

For just a few seconds we all fell silent, taken aback by this truly generous and unexpected gift. Our thoughts immediately turned to our little dog Candy, a West Highland terrier whom we had left in the care of Aunty Mary who absolutely adored her and who made a fuss of her whenever they visited us from their home in Darlington. Dad had said it was unfair to bring a Scottish dog into the heat of Malta and at about seven years old she would be better off staying in England. He was probably right but it was heartbreaking for Linda and me when the day of our parting had arrived.

Aunty Mary was of Flemish descent and was a widow with two children in Belgium in 1940. Uncle Frank, an elder brother of Dad and in the employ of British Intelligence working undercover, had been given the task of seeing her onto a British destroyer in Ostend before the entire country was overrun by invading Nazis. They must have clicked, because they were married soon afterwards. Mary was the loveliest, kindest lady who came from an aristocratic family in Flanders. I never knew her maiden name, but now I travel to the Bruges area several times each year and I often wonder if any of her family still live in that pleasant part of Belgium. The only thing I ever knew about them were that they had big connections with Sabena, the Belgian airline.

News of the Quality Street's arrival spread quickly and Aunty Joyce was a frequent caller. Her father, an amiable Glaswegian called Bob McKenzie, was by coincidence an agent for Quality Street in Scotland, earning several pence per tin sold north of the border. I recall that in the absence of television we played cards a lot and the prize was to close your eyes and pick out at random a sweet from the tin. I cheated. My favourites were the Brazil nuts coated in caramel and chocolate in a shiny purple wrapper. I practised so that I could feel the distinctive hump back nut shape even with my eyes shut.

Christmas came and went and 1961 arrived.

# 4.

None of us missed the English winter. Malta's winters were shirt sleeve weather and only rarely did you feel the need to wear a jumper. At weekends we took trips out in the Oxford, taking a picnic into the countryside. We generally stuck to the northern parts of the island, not just because they were nearer but because they had more hills and were thus more scenic.

One day we drove up a cart track as far as we could until we ran out of navigable road then walked the rest of the way uphill to a plateau called Wardija. Geographically it was directly opposite where we lived over the Bay and it was odd looking down to where we lived. Dad had bought a camping Gaz Bleu portable stove so wherever we picnicked a fresh brew of Lipton's tea was always the first priority, with a fag of course for Dad.

January and February could bring strong winds, usually from the northeast and the normally deep blue Mediterranean gave way to a snarling cauldron that cut into the soft natural limestone that had formed Malta's rocky and jagged coastline over many millennia. It was undoubtedly one of these tempests, that could often last for days, that led to the legend of St. Paul's shipwreck in the area that today bears his name.

Spring came early in March and the fields and roadsides were filled with the scent and colour of alfalfa, a daffodil type flower that Malta calls its own. Children would pick bunches of them to sell at the roadside for a few pennies. It was a short flowering season but it gave the signal that winter, such as it was, was over, and warmer days were coming. It was the signal for Dad to catch up on his horticulture.

We drove into Bur-Marrad and bought a mattock, a multi-purpose garden tool that was a cross between a spade and a hoe. Why they don't make them in England I will never know.It is the most useful garden tool ever invented and dates back to Biblical times. You could dig with it, hoe with it, rake with it and harvest with it as the task demanded. I was curious what Dad was going to do with it as we had no garden. I was soon to find out.

The next Saturday morning Dad and I climbed over the low stone wall which formed the boundary of Dolphin Flats. Next door was a large patch of waste ground where just a few weeds and some wild aniseed was growing. The land was fairly soft after some recent rain. Dad produced a longish piece of cord.

'Right, Mark, you grab this end and walk over to that wall over there.' I did.

Dad followed and produced a sturdy wooden stick about a foot long. Putting one end in the ground he banged the top end of it with the mattock until it was secure. He then tied one end of the cord to the stick as close to ground level as he could and then banged it again a few times for good measure. He then turned around and paying out the cord from the coil in his hand walked back to the wall. He banged the other stick in and tied the end of the cord to that one, tightening the line as he did so.

Now it dawned on me what he was doing. We had done this many times together on our allotment in Scarborough. Something was about to get sown, grown and eaten. But what? I was soon to find out but first we cleared all the vegetation using the mattock. It didn't take long. Dad disappeared into the flat and emerged a short while later with a brown bag full of small potatoes. Each one had one or more greenish shoots sticking out of it. Even at seven years old I was highly sceptical. Don't tell me we were going to grow our own spuds? Oh yes we were!

The row was a good thirty feet long I guess and a shallow trench about four inches deep and six inches wide was hewn into the soil using the mattock. Then the seed potatoes were gently placed at roughly one foot intervals into the trench, shoots pointing skyward. The loose topsoil was then raked carefully back on top of them all along the row. Job done. All we needed now was some rain. The question of planting permission had already been dealt with. The patch of land was owned by our genial landlords Charles and Walter Bezzina, two brothers from the town of Naxxar (Nash Are) the other side of Mosta. They intended to build more flats on the land when finances allowed.

Spring showers arrived within days and very soon the potatoes were showing shoots, then leaves, through the soil. Only a week had passed. In England I had been a keen helper of Dad in our allotment which was close to Scarborough's Open Air Theatre and although only seven I was well versed in the difference between earlies, middles and lates, a reference to when the potatoes in question could be expected to be cropped. I asked Dad if our new ones would be earlier than Arran Pilots, our potato of choice back home.

'Much earlier than that, Boy, if what I've been told is right,' was his response. Unbelievably, six weeks after planting we dug the first ones up, ready to eat. They weren't huge or particularly plentiful but they were almost snow white and tasted marvellous. But still Dad wasn't too happy.

'A chap at work, a local, has told me how to improve the yield so we'll try another row.'

You couldn't do that in England or Scotland from where Arran Pilots derived their origin. The growing season just isn't long enough and you only get one shot, as it were. But it turned out up to six crops a year is not uncommon in the fertile valleys in Malta.

Next weekend we went to a small beach in the extreme northeast of the island and raked loads of seaweed into several sacks and took them home. It wasn't the sort of seaweed you would expect to see in England but resembled fawn coloured ribbons four to six inches long. The beach was covered in it after recent high seas. The next day the trench was dug anew and more seed potatoes planted, but this time seaweed was placed in the trench for its entire length under and over all the spuds. The soil was raked back in and the line of cord removed.

Six weeks later we harvested a crop twice as heavy as the first and they tasted absolutely exquisite. The seaweed was a tip given to him by a gardener and handyman who worked at Dingli. We visited him one weekend to buy some zinnias and other plants for our balcony. He wouldn't take any money so Dad had bought him a bottle of VAT 69 whisky which he knew was his favourite tipple. It is the seaweed on the island of Jersey that gives Jersey Royals their special taste. You can't buy Maltese potatoes outside Malta: they are far too nice to export. Majorcan potatoes, which taste almost as nice, are to be found in good English greengrocers for a few weeks around March time but they are soon snapped up.

It was that spring when I had an accident at school. I fell off a climbing frame in the school playground. I probably only fell about five feet but the ground was as hard as rock. In fact it mostly *was* rock. I yelped as I fell on my left forearm which immediately didn't feel right and the duty school teacher, a Mrs Smith, came running over. She was by nature a brusque, overpowering person but was actually quite kind to me. I was taken to the headmaster's office. He was a slim, kindly man with a wispy moustache and gold-rimmed glasses. His name was Mr Ozouf which sounded as if he was Tutankhamen's second cousin but actually he was as English as I was.

He obviously didn't like the look of my arm which was starting to bruise up about four inches back from my left wrist. A medic was summoned from the adjacent St. Andrews Army barracks and it wasn't long before I was being properly examined by a professional. It wasn't good news. He thought my arm was fractured and I would have to go to hospital. Was I to go back to the hospital where I had been born eight years earlier? No: next stop was Bighi Military Hospital operated mainly by the Royal Navy.

For some reason I was taken by the school porter, a kindly Maltese gentleman, across the road to Jessie's Bar. A lady brought me a Coke and, of all things, a huge spam sandwich. An Army ambulance painted in khaki with a red cross on the side arrived and I was gently lifted up into the front seat with an orderly alongside me. With my good hand I clung on to the sandwich, and waited for the driver. He was ages coming. Maybe he was waiting for a spam sandwich too.

There is only one way to Bighi by road and it's the long way. It is situated on a high promontory on the south side of Grand Harbour. It would have been quicker to have gone by boat which is how thousands of wounded allied soldiers arrived there in the First World War. Looking back again to Sir Trevor McDonald's *Secret Mediterranean* he even pointed it out on his tour of the harbour. It featured an external electric lift which transported the casualties direct from boats more than a hundred feet up to waiting medical staff. Sadly many died there. By comparison my suspected broken arm was just a mere scratch.

The journey took for ever with every bounce and turn hurting my arm. We were there for over three hours during which my arm was examined, X-rayed and then placed in a plaster cast from wrist to elbow. I felt terrible. My mum and dad didn't even know where I was as hardly anybody had telephones in those days. It was mid-afternoon by the time another Army vehicle took me home to XemXija which was about half-an-hour earlier than normal on a school day. The Oxford was parked outside.

I walked slowly down the twenty odd steps and tried to let myself in. The door was shut and locked. I knocked and shouted, but no-one came. I was really upset. It seemed like only one other family in the block was at home. They were called Stan and Sheila Johnstone. They were from Hartlepool, and Stan was a colleague of Dad's but maybe ten or more years older. They had no kids but did have a lovely cocker spaniel called Timmy who Linda and I took walking as often as we wanted to. Thus Timmy became a substitute for the dog we had left behind in Scarborough.

Sheila took me inside and made me a cup of tea. She told me that my parents and Maurice and Joyce had all gone up to Mellieha Bay where the men wanted to practise their golf swings. This was news to me. I didn't even know that Dad had brought his old set of clubs from England out with him. Maurice's Wolseley came purring into the top car park at the same time as we would normally have got back from school. Mum was horrified as she stared at me with my left arm in plaster.

'Oh, Mark, what have you done?'

I went to school the next day as normal and found myself to be quite the little hero. Everybody in the class wanted to sign the plaster and very soon there was no room left. I was excused sports for the next month which didn't concern me too much as the so called football pitch was just solid earth and baked hard by a powerful Mediterranean sun. There wasn't a blade of grass in sight at any time of the year, not even when it rained.

The sports teacher made a flag for me using drawing pins to affix a handkerchief onto a stick and appointed me the linesman for all games I should have played in. I must have looked a right tosser running up and down with the flag in one hand and the other coated in plaster and held up with a sling. I was slated for getting a couple of offside decisions wrong but to be honest I didn't really understand what that meant at the time. Not sure I do even now.

In early May, just after the start of the summer term, Dad announced that we were going on a week's holiday to Naples in southern Italy, though without Linda who was considered too young at six years old. I was excited. How big would the ship be, I wondered, as images of *Queen Mary* leapt into my imagination.

'We're not going by sea. It would take too long. We're going to fly there and back on a BEA Vickers Vanguard.'

I was disappointed and excited at the same time. I still hadn't set foot on anything that floated that was bigger than a rowing boat in Scarborough's Peasholm Park. Considering I was a sailor's son I thought that was a poor show. I would just have to wait.

The day of departure arrived. It was a Saturday and Stan Johnstone kindly took us to Luqa Airport with two suitcases. We saw the plane from some distance away and it looked like a bigger version of the Viscount to me which is exactly what it was. It looked resplendent in its black, red and white livery. We were soon airborne as Luqa in those days probably had about six civil air movements a day as opposed to a hundred plus today. I sat between Mum and Dad as Dad had bagged the window seat. Not fair. He did swap seats with me before we came into Naples and I got my first view of a volcano as I saw Mount Vesuvius as we circled the city before landing. A car met us and took us to our hotel, the Albergo Patria.

I will not dwell in this story of the seven days in Naples and its surrounds. As a condition of taking a week off school during term time Mr Ozouf had made me promise to keep a diary which he would inspect on my return to school.

'I want a proper diary mind you. Keep any train tickets, museum receipts and leaflets and stick them into this exercise book.'

He passed me a substantial maroon coloured book and it immediately dawned on me that I had better look sharp and remember everything and write it down at the end of every day. Dad had a great idea.

'Why don't we keep notes in a small pad and then write the diary up properly when we get back.'

So that's just what we did. I still have that diary to this day. Every evening after tea I wrote up the diary. *Day One. Took off by BEA Vanguard from Luqa* etc etc. I had saved the airline's advertising leaflet with a super photo of the plane so that was stuck in on the first page.

And so it went on. *Day Two. Visited the Roman City of Pompei buried by ash from Vesuvius in AD79* etc. etc. *Day Three. Took a ferry to Capri. Spotted Gracie Fields in her garden. Dad was impressed but I hadn't a clue who she was.* And so on, you get the general drift.

The whole thing took a lot longer than I thought and I got tired sometimes and made errors. It was a good job I was writing in pencil and a rubber eraser came in handy many a time. How many kids use pencils and rubbers today? Not many I'll warrant. It's ipads, smart phones and laptops and written English has become a predictive melange of cliches, sound-bites and meaningless catch phrases. LOL! See what I mean?

Anyway, perhaps a week after returning from Italy the diary was ready to present to Mr Ozouf. All that remained was to stick a photo of the Patria Hotel on the front cover. This proved to be a messy task as rather too much of that sticky gum shot out of the red plastic tip than intended and ended up on the dining room table. However the job was complete and amazingly Dad was happy with the end result.

The next morning, just before assembly, I knocked gingerly at the headmaster's door which was slightly ajar. It always was, I remember. The last time I had been in his office was when I had broken my arm.

'Come in, Mark.'

He must have spotted me coming. I proffered the now written up diary in the maroon book he had given me. We both remained standing as he swiftly thumbed through the book which was probably twice as thick now with the addition of all the museum tickets, ferry tickets to the islands of Ischia and Capri and all sorts of memorabilia from BEA. He was genuinely taken aback.

'My goodness me, you have been busy haven't you? I'll read it tonight and let you know what I think about it.'

The very next morning, just after class registration, there was a knock on the door and in came Mr Ozouf, my diary in his hand. Army schools were quite strict and the teacher boomed out:

'All stand for the headmaster!'

Mr Ozouf spoke a few quiet words to the teacher, faced us and told us to sit down.

'Mark has been with his family in Italy during term time and I granted him permission on condition he kept a diary. He kept his word and I am going to read the first section to you. *Day One.*' Etc etc.

I was so embarrassed! Looking back I guess it was my first book, but I had no notion or inkling of that at the time.

# 5.

The rest of that school year was uneventful. I had adjusted to life in a co-ed Army school and I was looking forward to being promoted to Class 2A after the next summer holidays. Mike Davis and I became firm school pals and I discovered that Mike had actually been born in Scarborough. He could so easily have been born in Ceylon as his father, Bob, had been posted to Colombo shortly after getting married to Beryl. I didn't see Mike much outside of school as his family lived in Sliema in Rudolf Street.

The other Michael, Mick Church, lived in Balzan so I didn't see much of him either. However another lad arrived in that year called Brian Carr and his family lived on the beach road about two hundred yards from Dolphin Flats. We got on famously. His father was Captain Paddy Carr, Royal Marines, and he was the Officer commanding the RM Training Camp at Ghajn Tuffieha on the coast about two miles west of St. Paul's Bay. I think they had to wait for Paddy's predecessor to vacate his official residence on the camp but as soon as they could they moved to Ghajn Tuffieha, often simply called Golden Bay.

I would often go and stay with the Carrs at weekends. We had the run of the whole camp. There was a NAAFI (Navy Army & Air Force Institute) to buy sweets and Coke and there was even a small cinema. However the main attraction, for Brian at least, was the assault course where you could swing across a huge ditch clinging for dear life to a rope, climb a replica of a ship's mast, crawl through a tunnel and do all sorts of things that boys like to do but shouldn't.

We built a tree house in a carob tree just behind their house but my affection for it disappeared altogether when an iron bar which was one of the main supporting lintels fell out while I was underneath it, crashing into my right ankle. The camp medic took a look at it and pronounced me fit for service but I swear that it has not been quite the same to this day.

The other huge advantage that the camp possessed was its own little harbour about half a mile away down a long winding path. It was known as Dory Harbour on account of the dory working boats stored there. In the summer they were always in the water and secured by lanyards to the jetty but in winter they were hauled out into a small covered yard where they were presumably painted and serviced. We were told that the Queen and Prince Philip used to bathe there when the Duke was stationed in Malta as a serving Naval officer. It would have been very private and secure indeed with a platoon of Marines probably guarding the cliff tops above them. The two dories were about fifteen feet long and powered by inboard petrol engines driving a single screw. Paddy took Brian and me out many times for a ride and let us take the tiller from time to time. They weren't very quick, probably about ten knots maximum, but they were great fun. One particular weekend Brian came up with the idea that we two might just sneak down to Dory Harbour and take the boats out on our own without telling anyone. We had watched Paddy start the engines often enough so why not. Try as we might the engines just would not start.

We didn't know it, but we had been spotted. Later in the day, I think over tea, Paddy said something like: 'You didn't really think the fuel tanks would be left full did you?' We cringed.

My parents and Brian's parents became great friends too. Paddy was originally from Harrogate although his Marines career took the family to many different places. They also had a daughter, Sonia, who was much older and who was at University in England. She often came out for holidays travelling on a BEA Comet, a jet plane that was much faster than the Viking, Viscount or Vanguards that were pedestrian in performance by comparison. I remember we went to Luqa to see her off after one holiday and the gleaming de Havilland Comet on the apron made other planes look like flying handcarts. The Memorandum of Understanding between the British and French Governments to develop the Concorde was about to be signed which in turn would make the Comet look dated.

For the first year at St. Andrew's my sister and I ate school dinners. These were taken at the NAAFI about three hundred yards away. At the blowing of the duty teacher's whistle, a long crocodile of kids would walk from the front gate of the school across the short adjacent road and down the side of the football pitch to the NAAFI building. I assumed that soldiers and marines ate there in the mornings and evenings but at lunchtimes from Monday to Friday it was effectively the school dining room. You queued up with a tray and staff would serve you your portions of whatever.

The only thing I remember clearly was that every Friday Russian fish pie was on the menu. What made it Russian I will never know. Forget any notion of salmon, prawns and smoked haddock in a white wine sauce topped with mashed Maris Piper and browned off with a Parmesan crust. This version of fish pie was chunks of a local fish, lampuki, surmounted by a well baked short crust pastry. Served with chips, peas and liberal applications of tomato sauce it was quite delicious to my palate. However it was deeply unpopular with most kids and I could always have a second helping if I wanted one. Lampuki was a seasonal fish caught locally and to me tasted not unlike herrings or kippers which I had been used to eating back in Scarborough. Russian fish pie was served every Friday, fifty-two weeks of the year, so the use of deep freezers was obviously common practice even back in 1960.

The lunches were purchased with a blue ticket which your parents had to buy in advance from any NAAFI and they cost one shilling each which at the time was not cheap. That equates to five pence today or about seven euro cents.

Our own family shopping was split between the local shops in St. Paul's Bay where we bought bread, fruit and Dad's Hop Leaf, and bigger shops in Sliema. Maybe every two weeks we would drive into Sliema to use the NAAFI at Tigne Barracks (pronounced Tee Nee). On our first trip there I was surprised to see quite a few heavy anti-aircraft guns parked outside, all painted a dark khaki with their long barrels pointing skywards. Dad said they were left there from the war. Looking back and thinking about it, the War had been over for fifteen years and the guns probably hadn't been fired in anger since about 1943. Somehow living in Malta was like living in a permanent war museum.

Apart from a couple of week's supply of NAAFI dinner tickets we would buy British food such as tinned peas, baked beans, HP sauce, Marmite and bacon. Fruit and veg we bought at local shops. The egg lady knocked at the door every few days and sold eggs individually from a big zinc bucket. The bigger the eggs the more expensive they were, ranging from one to three pennies each. Cracked eggs were all sold for a penny and Mum used to buy them to make cakes and sponges. Egg boxes didn't seem to have reached Malta yet. I often used to wonder if news that the War had ended had reached Malta either.

We didn't buy much, if any, fish, as the local cafés and restaurants served lots of it; although Malta was half starved of bread, flour, fruit and vegetables during the War it would never run out of seafood. Apart from my favoured lampuki there was dendici (a tender and succulent white fish not unlike sole in taste and texture), swordfish and tuna which the locals called tunny. The latter was often served in open sandwiches mixed with chopped olives and capers. It was called a ftir (foot ear is about as close as you can get phonetically). Delicious is all I can say.

As you might expect all local fruit and veg was seasonal. Water melons were almost given away and were complemented with honeydew and galia varieties too. Olives, both green and black, were plentiful and cheap. I have retained a predilection for both since those days. And of course olive oil was as common and plentiful as say lemonade in England. By the time I was eight I could tell the difference between three different brands with my eyes shut. Ollio Sasso which was sold in green pint tins was my favourite. Salad cream? Mayo? I don't think anyone in Malta had even heard of it in those days. And of course local potatoes were just magic including our own home grown ones. But of all Malta's crops tomatoes were and still are the most prevalent and delicious. There are simply fields and fields of them. No need for greenhouses and paraffin stoves here. They were mostly of the Italian plum type. They were tasty just on their own but thinly sliced, liberally drizzled with Ollio and sprinkled with salt they were simply yummy.

If all the above add up to what the 21$^{st}$ century health police call a Mediterranean diet then all I can say is 'bring it on'.

You had to be careful to thoroughly wash all locally grown vegetables. A particularly nasty dose of 'the squits' could be contracted out of the blue and lay you low for a couple of days. Dubbed Malta dog it was apparently caused by an excess of phosphates in the soil in certain areas of horticultural activity. Whether that was an excess of fertiliser or natural occurring phosphates I don't know. On balance I rather favour it was the latter as I cannot see Maltese farmers eking out a subsistence livelihood paying for fancy fertilisers.

I mentioned seafood and the abundance of seafood establishments. Our favourite was called the Harbour Bar in St. Paul's Bay and it was just a few yards from the church that commemorates his name and believed to be the first church constructed on the island, post-shipwreck one assumes. This restaurant had an unusual feature. Carved into the rock outside was a pool full of sea water with an outlet/inlet to the open sea. It was about six feet deep and maybe fifteen feet square. Around the perimeter were iron railings with many lengths of heavy duty cord securely tied to them, the other ends disappearing into the water. At the other end of each cord, clinging equally tightly, would be a live lobster. The intending diner simply pulled one up, decided whether or not it was to his or her liking in size, and notified the waiter who then took it to the chef. A few Hop Leafs or a Martini on the verandah later the newly cooked crustacean was served up with salads, hopefully phosphate free, and all was well with the culinary world. Animal rights didn't get a look in then and probably still don't today. They weren't cheap though. I probably had to make do with a ftir. Oh well.

# 6.

In the summer holiday I gave up fishing and learnt to swim at long last. I was not a natural swimmer and it was a long time before I finally discarded the rubber ring and inflated armbands. It made days at the beach a much more adventurous affair. Our favourite beach was called Little Armier, about four miles north as the crow flies except there are no crows in Malta. In fact very little flies in Malta, such is the obsession with hunting down the island's birdlife.

To get to Little Armier you drove north via Mellieha and headed for the Gozo ferry terminal which was then at Marfa and turned right past the bigger Armier Beach and headed east on a dirt track as far as you could go. You knew you were almost there when you passed the one of those wind driven water pumps driven by a that in the absence of moving air was donkey driven with a or without the carrot in front of its nose. The last couple of hundred yards must have been agony for the car's suspension and you had to make sure you stopped before the cart track turned into you got stuck in the sand of the beach itself. Getting stuck on hot dry sand would have needed the Army to pull you out.

We went to this beach nearly every day that Dad had a day off work. The Boys worked a peculiar shift system including one night shift every four days but the upside was plenty of day-time to go to the beach. Moss and Joyce invariably joined us, sometimes with the Knockolds family. Brian Knockolds was an RAF man and their daughters Susan and Pat were great fun. They were excellent swimmers and by comparison I was a mere floating brick. However my performance was soon enhanced when Dad bought me a pair of flippers from a sports shop in Tower Road.

Unfortunately instead of buying me the blue flippers that everybody else seemed to use he bought me some black ones. So what? Well the difference was that the black ones were made from a heavier type of rubber that was denser than sea water and they didn't float. That didn't matter if one accidentally came off in a few feet of water but once one came off when I was swimming in about a depth of ten feet. Moss saved the day by duck-diving to retrieve the flipper from the sandy bottom but a stern lecture from Dad followed.

Aqua-dynamically speaking the flippers were a great success and probably added a knot to my best normal speed of half a knot. With Dad being ex-Navy all speeds, even on land, were measured in knots even though the Oxford's speedo was calibrated in miles per hour. In a similar fashion all floors were called decks and all walls bulkheads. It drove my mum crazy but actually I quite liked it. To this day I still say 'knots' and if you think about it a nautical mile of 2,000 yards is far simpler than a statute mile of 1,760 yards. Whoever dreamt that one up? It does make you wonder.

Sadly the flippers only lasted about half the summer holiday and like an isotope they had a 'half-life' probably of about four weeks. I was swimming off the side of a boat when somehow one came off and sank to the bottom, maybe about thirty feet below. I was inconsolable and Dad was livid. He did not buy me a replacement so for the rest of the summer I swam at about one knot in circles as I did a passable imitation of the *Bismarck* when it was torpedoed and its rudder jammed.

Little Armier Beach was always quiet. Any other users were invariably Service families as the local buses didn't run further than the main Armier Beach. The channel between the north of Malta and the island of Comino was deep and straight and the beach faced it. On numerous occasions we watched a small flotilla of Royal Navy destroyers in line astern charging through the channel at what looked like maximum speed, probably about thirty-five knots. The resultant waves would hit the beach for several minutes after they had passed and it was great fun to ride them in on a Lilo.

The water was always crystal clear and we could see the sea bed below at a depth of thirty feet or more. Unfortunately every so often small balls of lumpy, sticky tar would wash in. These were the result of oil tankers cleansing their tanks and flushing them out with sea water. Since those days maritime rules have changed and they are not allowed to do it close to land. Accidentally standing on one of those tar balls was not funny as it took ages to remove it from the soles of our feet. Not to mention a *How many times have I told you to be careful* reminder from a glaring parent.

The Mediterranean sun is fierce, particularly in July and August, and we used beach tents to provide shade and a modesty screen when the ladies were changing. It wasn't the traditional diagonal shaped tent but more of a square canvas box with a six foot pole at each corner. Guy ropes, two each per corner, ensured the four poles stayed vertical; regularly, people didn't spot them and came crashing down onto the hot sand.

Our second favourite beach was Paradise Bay which faced northwest and was the other side of the Gozo ferry terminal. Its main drawback was that the only access, other than by boat, was by a zillion steps from a car park at the summit. The effort was worth it, I always thought, as the water there is as clear as gin. At the foot of the steps was a small café that sold cold drinks which did a roaring trade at weekends especially. On the very last time we ever went there some workmen had just finished concreting the last few steps which took you from the path onto the beach. Dad looked at the box underneath the permanently mounted bottle opener which caught the metal bottle tops of scores of Cokes, 7 Ups and Pepsis. Then he looked back at the still unset concrete and looked at me.

'Are you thinking what I'm thinking?'

I was, so we did.

We took about fifty bottle tops from the catchment box and laid them out, shiny side up, on the bottom step until they spelt out the football team we both followed.

S P U R S

We then very carefully stood gently on each letter until the tops were nicely secured in their new concrete home. Then we legged it. To this day I have never been back to see if our tribute is still there. With apologies to the Maltese Environment Agency. Sorry. Perhaps we should have spelt out Sliema Wanderers but that's an awful lot of letters and an awful lot of bottle tops.

Little Armier and Paradise Bay were the only two beaches that we used regularly. Golden Bay, adjacent to the Marines' Camp at Ghajn Tuffieha, was a nice sandy beach but as it was on a bus route it was always packed at weekends. In any case Dory Harbour in the company of the Carrs was always the number one choice in that part of the island with a nice cuppa brewed by Joan before we headed off back in the Oxford to XemXija.

As you might expect the spelling of where we lived was a pen twister as well as a tongue twister. Letters and birthday cards received from friends and relatives in England produced an infinite number of combinations and variations. Letters were always addressed Malta G.C. in those days, not just plain Malta. It was like the island's own trademark. Woe betide anybody who left off the GC. The island had earned that medal the hard way with blood, sweat and tears and nobody was going to take it away from them.

To cut down on the actual writing of letters between us and the grandparents in Scarborough, Dad had come up with a terrific idea. We would post tapes back and forth to each other. You could get so much more news even on a small three inch tape than on any letter or blue Aerogram as they were called then. Thus about a month before he left Scarborough for Malta Dad bought a small Philips tape recorder and a supply of three inch tapes. They were the smallest you could buy and gave about fifteen minutes' playing time. There were going to be several dummy runs before Granny got the hang of it. Grandad left her to it, being more concerned with his tomatoes, chrysanthemums or whatever required his attention in the garden department.

The arrival of a tape from the grandparents was always a cause of excitement. We usually waited until after tea then Dad would set up our tape recorder, a small Grundig. He would place it on a coffee table, the power flex trailing from a two pin plug in a wall socket, and we would all sit around agog. Dad would put the newly arrived tape on the left side spool and carefully wind the leader tape through the playback head and onto the empty collecting reel.

'Are we all ready then? Switching on now. All quiet.'

Grandma had just a slight speech impediment – not a stammer or a stutter, but just a slight hesitation and invariably the monologue started with something like this. She was fine once she got going.

'Hel... hel... hello everybody. Here we are again then. We're all well here... hope you are too. Your dad's at the cricket, Hylda, Yorkshire against somebody I just forget now. Thought I'd start this while he's out. You know how awkward he can be when I ask him to say a few words into this thing! He dries up as soon as I put the microphone thingy under his nose.'

And so she would chatter on about how busy the town was when she was shopping, who she had seen for coffee, how the aunties were, how well the garden looked and of course the weather. There was always news about the weather. How cold it was. How sunny it was. How windy it was. You could always tell when Grandad was about to speak. Invariably Granny would say:

'Now I'll just see if your dad's here... just a minute... Walter!... Walter!'

There would be ten seconds of silence followed by a sharp thump as Grandad rattled the microphone. He invariably started with the same opening words.

'Now then. Now then. I hope you can hear me alright? I'll never get the hang of this bloomin' thing.'

His news would be how well (or badly) Yorkshire were doing in their current match, if it was summer. If it was winter it would usually be news about his hopes for the Chrysanthemum Show that took place at Scarborough's Olympia. He was a frequent prizewinner but the cash prize of just a few shillings was a poor return for money spent on paraffin for his greenhouse lamp. His exhibits were mollycoddled for weeks in the run up to the Show itself.

The last minute of every tape was always a bit chancy as they tried to guess how many minutes or seconds were left on the spool. On several occasions we heard a cry of:

'Walter, you'd best be quick I don't think there's much tape...' then silence. Too late!

For the cost of the airmail postage, about two shillings, it was a wonderful and innovative way of keeping in touch. Nobody had phones in those days but in many ways those tapes were so much more exciting. We would all save news and stories for the next tape we sent back.

# 7.

The summer came and went and the sun-scorched days gave way to pleasanter climes. The new school term started in the September and we all moved up a year, me to Class 2A which meant a new form teacher in the shape of a Mr Manning.

He was very strict from day one. It was now *Sir* not *Mr* anything and he had a nasty but I suppose well meaning method of punishment for almost all misdemeanours. Our desks were the old fashioned ones that were fixed to a bench seat. The desk was at an angle towards you to facilitate easier writing and reading but the downside was that if you inadvertently left a pencil on the desk it rolled onto the floor, invariably breaking the lead in the pencil at the same time. Manning took this as an opportunity to learn as well as punish. He had ears like a bat's and as soon as he heard a pencil fall to the tiled floor he would point to the culprit and boom out:

'Kindness to pencils week!'

The pupil responsible for this heinous crime had to forfeit his or her play break and stay in the classroom to write all the multiplication tables from one to twelve. By the end of the first couple of weeks everybody had fallen foul of this crime but, boy, did we know our tables! Manning also had a reputation of being handy with a cane which he kept in the cupboard. Looking back I think he must have been something of a sadist and one poor chap in another class seem to get caned almost every week.

I was caned once during the whole year, and that wasn't really my fault. A classmate, Adrian Olsen, made the mistake of bringing his toy crossbow into school. It was made of green metal and fired a wooden arrow with a rubber sucker on the end to ensure that no damage was done to any target, intended or otherwise. William Tell was all the rage at the time and Adrian persuaded me to try and emulate his success. Taking an apple from his lunch box Adrian strode about twenty paces away from me and placed the apple on his head. He screwed his eyes up and said 'Fire!'

I took aim and pulled the trigger hoping that the arrow wouldn't be too accurate. I needn't have worried. A gust of wind arrived at the most unfortunate moment possible and took it way off course. Bad luck would have it that Mr Manning was the duty playground teacher and against all odds the bolt, sucker first, landed plumb into the cup of coffee he was holding at the time. Brown splashes erupted all over the front of his crisp white shirt.

'Come here boy!'

Did he mean me or Adrian? I had the crossbow in my hand. Talk about a smoking gun. Manning thought I was the owner. He grabbed it with both hands and bent it almost double.

'Six strokes, boy. See me at lunchtime.' It was the only time I ever got the cane at any of the six schools I attended in my life.

Educationally speaking Manning was a good teacher, though. Arithmetic became fractions and decimals and English became paragraphs and essays. I always got good marks for essays. He once gave me ten out of ten for *A Day out in Malta with the family*. My day was a day at Dory Harbour so it was a good job Brian Carr chose a different topic lest our stories didn't match. That particular day was the only time I ever saw a snake in Malta as it scuttled across the path from left to right about twenty yards ahead of us. It was probably frightened. Years later, thinking back, I remembered that St. Paul was supposed to have banished all snakes from the island having been bitten by one soon after his shipwreck. You have to careful with these legends. They can be deceptive. Ask William Tell.

It was around this time that one of the regular tapes from Granny gave us some welcome news: 'And we've got our flights booked to M... M... Malta.'

Mum was just so happy. We all were. Plans were made about what we would do, where we would go. And best of all they were going to be here for Christmas. I knew it would mean sharing a bedroom for several weeks with Linda: it didn't bother me, but I don't think she was too happy. Moss and Joyce were delighted too; back in Scarborough they had only lived five doors apart at numbers one and eleven Stepney Road. Moss kept chickens in his back garden and fresh eggs were regularly exchanged for fresh veg, in particular Grandad's famous Ailsa Craig tomatoes. Quite how a variety of tomato ever got named after a rocky island in the Firth of Clyde was always a mystery to me I must admit.

The day of the grandparents' arrival finally arrived in early December. I think it must have been a Saturday because I wasn't at school. It was around lunchtime and having parked the Oxford in the car park we positioned ourselves on the public viewing balcony at the air terminal. We watched as the BEA Vickers Viscount landed then taxied slowly to the apron and came to a standstill port side facing us. It was only some fifty yards away and we would get a great view of Granny and Grandad as they disembarked. Today's jet engines spool down in just a few seconds but yesteryears' turboprops took much longer and it was ages before the last of the four propellers fluttered slowly to a standstill. Finally some ground crew pushed a mobile flight of steps to the plane's door just behind the cockpit. The door swung open and the steps were made secure.

We could see some cabin crew bidding farewell to passengers as they disembarked but in those days they were probably spared the clichéd *have a nice day* that so infuriates me today. We watched and waited and waited. About fifty passengers got off but not Granny and Grandad. Our hearts fell. Where were they? If they had missed the plane we would have received a telegram by now. We watched, horrified, as a BEA ground hostess emerged from the building beneath our feet and pushed a wheelchair towards the plane steps. Suddenly Granny appeared at the aircraft's door clutching the arm of a stewardess. She looked up, saw the four of us on the balcony, and waved. She was well it seemed, thank goodness. She came down the steps holding a rail with one hand the stewardess with the other until she reached terra firma. Grandad followed a few steps behind. She waved again from the wheelchair and appeared cheerful.

Several minutes later in the passenger lobby she explained to us that she'd had one of her funny turns and it was nothing to worry about. The BEA crew had rightly erred on the side of caution. We were all overjoyed to see each other. It had been sixteen months since we had left Scarborough. The tapes had helped to shorten the distance between us but you can't beat a hug from your grandma.

The Oxford was squeezed full as I sat in the front with Mum and Dad, the bench seat proving its worth, with one leg either side of the gear lever. It had been eight years since their last visit. Grandad, with his farming background, made passing comments about the land looking a bit dry. It was a good forty minutes' drive to XemXija and Dolphin Flats and a nice cup of tea was the first priority after taking two large cases from the boot. They couldn't believe how big our flat was compared to the previous one they had seen in Spinola. But of course the family was bigger now, Dad a grade or two higher in seniority and the commensurate rent allowance a little more generous.

The next day Dad sprung a surprise on Grandad – and me too for that matter.

'Right, Walter, today we are going to plant some potatoes.'

The look on Grandad's round Yorkshire face was priceless.

'You can't plant taties in December, lad. They'll rot off int ground.'

Shortly after breakfast Dad led Grandad to the stone wall that separated us from the patch of ground next door that we had turned into an impromptu allotment. Dad had obviously been busy and the row had already been prepared. Grandad watched incredulously as Dad placed the seed potatoes in the shallow trench, raking in some seaweed before covering with the loose soil. I have no idea what went through Grandad's mind, but plainly he wasn't best pleased with the timing. Gardening, like cricket, just wasn't done on a Sunday.

It was school as usual the next day and of course for the next five days but when Saturday arrived it was picnic time as the weather was holding up beautifully. This was Dad's third tour to Malta in his Admiralty job and he knew just about every road on the island. We headed off via St. Paul's Bay and Bur-Marrad in the general direction of Mtarfa, the huge clock tower acting as a navigational beacon. We turned off towards an area known as the Chadwick Lakes which were used as reservoirs in bygone years. Finding a decent spot to pull off the road, deck chairs were assembled and of course the Campinggaz was lit and the kettle filled. Some things never change when English people are abroad.

We were probably halfway through cheese sandwiches and hard boiled eggs when a strange noise started coming our way. Gobble gobble! Gobble gobble! We couldn't believe it. It was a flock of turkeys accompanied by two young children probably about eight or nine years old and a teenage girl about thirteen or so. She spoke a little English and was very friendly. A seasonal thought immediately went through Dad's mind.

'Can we buy one of your turkeys to eat for Christmas?'

And that's how we came to meet the Azzopardi family. I cannot remember the girl's name but I'll call her Maria, which it probably was anyway. Maria took us to meet her family at their house which was actually only a few hundred yards away but off the road. We were stunned to find that the farmhouse was in fact a deep cave in a large limestone outcrop. There seemed to be two or maybe three generations living there. Inside it was cavernous – excuse the pun, but so it was. There were several 'rooms' with tables and beds and paraffin lamps everywhere as there was no electricity. The head of the family spoke to Dad with Maria acting as interpreter. A deal was done. Dad would collect the turkey, which would be plucked and gutted two days before Christmas and the price would be one pound. The men shook hands and with a wave and a smile we trekked back to the car. It was totally surreal. Grandad said he thought it was a rum do' but Yorkshire folk think lots of things are a rum do.

Over the next couple of weeks we did what we always did in the run up to Christmas. Christmas cake was baked and puddings made. As a Women's Institute member, Granny was a great help to Mum. It was just like the old days. Goodness knows what she would have thought of today's Calendar Girls posing for photographs with two cherry buns hiding their bare boobs.

I think Grandad got a bit bored but at least it was a lot warmer than Scarborough which by now would be cold and dark as the winter solstice and the shortest day approached. He was a common sight to the locals as he walked down the beach road, walking stick in hand, pausing awhile to sit on a stone wall and smoke a Sun Valley roll-up.

Dad and I went to collect the turkey on the appointed day and Mum sent a tin of home-made mince pies for the Azzopardi family. Dad was offered a nip of some liquid in a small glass, probably whisky. The entire family seemingly turned out to see us. We promised to call again in the New Year. The turkey seemed good and was nicely plucked and placed in several layers of greaseproof paper, secured in a cardboard box. We had a huge fridge at home and space had already been made for it. It was going to be a joyous Christmas with the six of us all together. We didn't know it at the time, but it was also going to be the last.

Christmas Day was warm and sunny. Spending Christmas in the Mediterranean is an absolute joy. The combination of warm weather and festive joy provides an ambience that is hard to beat. Did we miss the dark nights, the cosy fires and the Queen's speech on TV? Er, no, actually we didn't. Today the last item is 'trailed' and leaked so much in advance it is like watching a re-run in colour of the *Forsyte Saga*.

Once again our flat was full of callers including some who lived in Sliema. The Hendersons, Bill and June, knew Grandma from their own days in Scarborough and made a special effort to visit. I suspect that the mince pies were an added incentive. Jimmy Stewart, the Gateshead lad, and his Maltese wife Mary, also turned up for pies and sherry. It was a warm and happy, happy day. A Duchess Class locomotive arrived for me from Father Christmas and all was well with the world.

The fresh turkey from the Azzopardi family tasted as good as any English turkey – *Bootiful* as the late Bernard Matthews would have said. We decided to pay them another visit while the grandparents were still here. Grandad was given the honour of carving the bird which he did with total aplomb after theatrically sharpening the Sheffield made carving knife against the matching steel. As the first slice of the breast flopped aside, held on only by the crispiest of golden skin, he said: 'Bah, you can tell it's not one of them frozen yans way t'meat comes off t'blade.'

(He repeated the exercise two years later with the same words. What he didn't know was that the turkey on that occasion was in fact a frozen one. I was sworn to secrecy on pain of death).

The lunch was washed down with a bottle of red wine that had been produced and bottled by the father of our maid, Maria, who was in her early twenties and lived in the village of Mistra about a mile north. Dad said it was undrinkable which was not like him at all. He produced from the fridge a bottle of white wine labelled simply *Mistra White* and it was quite nice. I was allowed to drink wine if it was mixed fifty-fifty with water so I settled for that. For the time being anyway.

As I recall there were only two other local wines available at that time: a red called Lacryma Christi and a white called Lacryma Vita, the Tears of Christ and the Tears of Life respectively. These wines were made in Malta but the grapes would have been imported from the Naples region in Italy. Today, wine in Malta is a totally different story as I will come to later.

We had a few rainy days which pleased Dad no end as it favoured the growth of his row of potatoes over the wall which Grandad had probably forgotten about altogether. Every few days Dad would take a peek to see how they were coming along and he kept me up to speed.

'They'd better be ready before he goes back to England. I want to surprise him. I know he doesn't believe me!'

We had lots of trips out for picnics to here, there and everywhere. In general the weather was kind although when a cold spell does come along you really felt it as the floors were all tiled and heating rudimentary. No wonder Malta and its sister island Gozo are famous for their goat's wool jumpers and cardigans.

We had one of those Aladdin paraffin stoves that resembled a green metal upside down funnel. It was lit with matches and you could turn the black wick up or down to adjust the flame and hopefully the heat coming from it. The wick had to be cleaned every time it was lit. It was a filthy job and involved placing a circle of metal over the circular wick and turning it round and round umpteen times until all the black carbon was removed. It was not unlike an indoor barbecue except you weren't cooking anything. Having said that, the stove was used several times when the gas bottle for the oven had run out and the replacement had not yet arrived. The word *bottle* was something of a misnomer. They were large blue cannisters of gas, like industrial versions of the small blue Gaz stoves used for picnics. Ordering a new one to replace the outgoing one was not a precise science. Lifting it up by the strong metal handles gave you an indication as to how much was left but it was only an indication. On several occasions Yorkshire puddings failed to rise when the gas ran out mid-cooking. You ordered and paid for them at an office in Zachary Street, Valletta, and they would be delivered a couple of days later. We always tried to keep a spare handy but sometimes it just didn't work out. Sod's law again.

Granny had booked open return tickets with BEA and we knew, that by the end of January, Grandad would start to get a bit twitchy. His mind would soon be turning towards sowing the first of his seeds in the large greenhouse at Stepney Road. Sure enough after tea on the 1st February, exactly as Dad had predicted to me on the QT, Grandad drained the last of his tea and said: 'Well, it's been grand to see you all and we've had a lovely time haven't we, Maude, but I think it's time we started to think about the trip home. There's seeds to sow and...'

Dad just winked at me and I stifled a grin. Dad had potatoes on his mind, not seeds.

The day before they left Dad and I ventured over the wall, mattock in hand. The potatoes had flowered which was a good sign. We unearthed the first root. There were about six potatoes all about the size of a half-crown. They were again almost white with not a blemish on them. Percy Thrower himself would have approved. We dug up about six roots and Dad told me what he had in mind. I forget what we ate but whatever it was it was accompanied by generous helpings of those new potatoes, boiled and covered liberally with Anchor butter.

Grandad was truly amazed when he was told they were the ones we had planted the day after his arrival. It was just over six weeks ago. He was even more staggered when we produced a huge bag of them to take home to England on the plane the next day. It would no doubt have been another rum story to tell his horticultural friends when he got home.

The day of departure arrived. We took Granny and Grandad to Luqa Airport in the late afternoon for a take off time of about six o'clock as I remember. Goodbyes were said and tears were shed. It would be another eighteen months before we all met again. We didn't wait to see the plane take off as it was almost dark anyway. The drive back to XemXija was in almost total silence. It was just awful. At about 6.15 we first heard the BEA Viscount as it clawed its way up into the sky almost over our heads as it headed northwest towards Gozo then the open sea. Soon we could clearly see the flashing red and green navigation lights on the wing-tips, red on the port side, green to starboard.

'Don't forget, Boy,' Dad was always reminding me, 'a bottle of port is red. You can't forget that.'

I didn't either. It was another bit of naval parlance in my blood.

# 8.

Soon after Christmas, Morris and Joyce announced that they had decided to move into town – Sliema, to be precise. Joyce just loved shops and there weren't many in St. Paul's Bay. Not the sort that Joyce liked anyway! They moved to Navarino Flats on Tower Road overlooking the sea and facing northeast. Mum was upset, as she and Joyce were great friends. I thought at the time that it would only be a matter of time before Mum wanted to move too.

I remember some reconstruction work being done at the side of our flats. A new flight of steps was being constructed right outside our kitchen window. When completed it would allow for everybody, not just the ground floor, to walk down to the beach road for a dip and it avoided a four hundred yard detour. Two builders arrived one day, one driving a small truck the other a very posh car indeed. Dad told me it was a Humber Hawk. It looked odd.

They rigged up a few wooden planks and secured them with ropes near to the top of the existing flight of steps and then proceeded to build a chute made entirely of these planks until it stretched down about thirty feet. I watched and just couldn't believe what they did next. Large pieces of pre-cut stone were simply manhandled by one of the men onto the top of the chute and let go. The angle was probably about thirty degrees to the horizontal. The stone slab then accelerated on its merry way until it was physically arrested at the bottom by the second man.

Somehow, though, they didn't look like workmen and they were quite tidy with their sleeves rolled up. I was amazed when Mum took some coffee out to them and started chatting. They were none other than our landlords, Charles and Walter Bezzina. They were, I'm guessing, in their early fifties at the most and had apparently made their money on the Queensland sugar plantations. They were cheery chappies and they invited Dad and me to attend the Malta Trade Fair at Naxxar where they lived. It was the first time I ate rabbit or fenek as it is called locally. Fried in olive oil with garlic and red and green peppers it tasted good. It is often described as Malta's national dish but as it is eaten in many countries I would tend to dispute that. If asked to nominate a candidate for that title I would opt for the pasta based timpana. Like a lot of things, it's all a matter of opinion.

With Moss and Joyce now living in Sliema our own trips into town became more frequent and the first time I stepped into Navarino Flats I was surprised to bump into a classmate called Heather Prince who lived there too. Her father, Wally, was another of Dad's colleagues who had also served in Melbourne, Australia. It had been a narrow shave as to whether Dad was posted there in 1952 after getting married. Mum was relieved it was Malta not Melbourne as there'd have been no chance of her parents visiting Down Under. And come to think of it I would have been born in Melbourne too and my life would probably have taken a very different course.

Heather was a little sweetie as were several other girls in my class. There had been a new input at the beginning of the school year which was common in Forces Schools when Army Regiments moved, Squadrons were formed up or disbanded and Royal Naval units deployed elsewhere in what was left of a dwindling Empire. Some kids, mainly Army offspring, spent weeks on end in transit, waiting for accommodation in Cyprus, Singapore or Hong Kong, not to mention West Germany where at the time the BAOR (British Army of the Rhine) was bigger than the whole of the Army today.

All the new kids were very pleasant. Geoffrey Barnes from Leytonstone, East London, arrived. He was a good chess player and he supported Spurs too! Reginald Parmenter was a good swimmer – almost as good as Mike whose genes must have included a throwback to the days when we were all aquatic mammals. Monica Hall was a tiny little brunette who wore glasses and spoke English as if she was taking elocution lessons. She was as quiet as a mouse so quite why she was chosen to read a lesson at the Christmas carol service I will never know. Brian Carr, the boy who was chosen, had a voice that could be heard from a great distance without a microphone. I think the only bit of Monica's lesson we could hear was the *Thanks be to God* at the very end.

Two other girls I recall very well indeed. One was Evelyn Wilson, a pretty Scottish girl who supported Partick Thistle. The other was a stunningly attractive girl called Caroline Galloway. She had long shiny black hair and a permanent smile. She was the daughter of an eminent Army dental surgeon, a Major General. Quite by chance some forty years later I just happened to see his obituary in the *Daily Telegraph*. It brought back a lot of memories. All of them good.

As in most schools, pupils were split into Houses for sporting and competitive purposes. At St. Andrew's they were named after WW2 Army heroes: Alexander, Gort, Wavell and Montgomery. These were represented by the colours blue, yellow, green and red. I was in Alexander which was fine by me as blue was my favourite colour at the time. So we all wore ties in the colour of our House – well, in the winter anyway: in summer nobody wore a tie as it was simply too hot.

General Gort was a man of great passion and humanitarian concern as well as being a fighting soldier: he won a Victoria Cross in the 1914-18 War. He was Governor of Malta during most of the siege of 1942/3 as Italy and Germany tried to bomb Malta and its terrified civilian population into submission.

If you control Malta, in particular the Grand Harbour, you can control the whole of the Mediterranean. With food and fuel supplies dwindling by the day it broke Gort's heart every time he had to announce yet another cut in rations. He was Malta's Churchill, but in 21st century England when most school kids think Churchill is a toy bulldog, what chance is there for Gort to be remembered?

Deliverance from the siege came with the arrival of four cargo ships and an oil tanker, the five survivors of a convoy three times that number that had set out from Gibraltar. There had been a catastrophic loss of men and ships, in particular the aircraft carrier *Eagle*. The remnants limped into Malta on the 13th and 14th of August under their own steam, the *Brisbane Star* with its bows almost blown off. Badly damaged by enemy bombs *Ohio* had been abandoned and re-boarded twice by its Master and crew. It simply refused to sink. Lashed to the destroyers *Penn* and *Ledbury*, one on each beam, *Ohio* arrived in Grand Harbour on the 15th – the feast of Santa Maria, sometimes called the Feast of the Assumption. So who's a non-believer now?

Thus the names of the *Rochester Castle, Port Chalmers, Brisbane Star, Melbourne Star* and the awe inspiring tanker *Ohio* have passed into Malta's history in the same manner that Kings and Queens have done in England. The Master of the *Ohio*, Captain Dudley Mason, was awarded the George Cross.

You don't get a G.C. for being a time serving, superannuated tosser in the Civil Service. You only get it for supreme gallantry. And that's why Sir William Dobbie, Gort's predecessor as Governor, accepted the George Cross for the Island of Malta. Gort was one of the most decorated Englishmen in history but the Sword of Honour conferred on him by the people of Malta was arguably the ultimate in personal chivalry.

So the school was run on almost military lines. How could it be otherwise? Army buses took us to Robb Lido at St. George's Bay for swimming lessons. Certificates of merit were awarded for distances swum, on the surface or under it, metres dived from a board (or possibly feet in those days) and depths duck-dived. This was my least favourite, probably because it brought back memories of the lost black flipper. We all had annual medicals by the Medical Officer who checked whether our nuts were descending and whether we could see straight. I had twenty twenty vision in those days. I think we all did with the exception of little Monica. We were also handed tablets in the summer months to compensate for salt lost when perspiring. Today salt is public enemy number one as far as the health police are concerned. So who's got it right?

Regular school trips were organised to places of interest but to be honest they were of more interest to historians than your average nine year old. Trips to catacombs and pre-Christian mesozoic ruins didn't rate terribly highly in the popularity charts. On the other hand visits to a cigarette factory (I tried to pinch some for Dad) and the Coca-Cola bottling plant were good days out. Another trip was to St. John's Co-Cathedral in Valletta.

I had joined the St. Andrew's Scouts, or more accurately, the Wolf Cubs, a sort of wholly owned subsidiary you might say. Fortunately for me the Grand Mufti (Akela or Lone Wolf) was none other than Captain Carr which meant that I got a lift to the weekly meetings every Tuesday evening after school. I guess there were about twenty odd Cubs in the pack and I started off as a junior Cub in Brown Six. All the Sixes were named after colours. Brian was in Black Six. I swiftly took proficiency badges in such noble arts as Observer, Medic and other Scouting activities like woodcraft although, with the lack of woods in Malta, desert survival would have been more appropriate.

It was good fun and Brian and I took it all a stage further by borrowing radio sets from the Marines' Camp. We probably resembled a Junior *Dad's Army* by the time we'd done it all. We fashioned our woggles from all sorts of material and perhaps the most unusual one I had was made from a chunk of bone from a leg of long ago eaten lamb. Hollowed out and highly polished it looked almost like a piece of ivory when the sun shone on it. Goodness knows what the lamb would have thought of having a chunk of its leg utilised in this fashion. There was great competition amongst us for the best woggles but I always thought my bone one was the best.

Sometimes after the usual exercises and *Dyb dyb dybs* and *Dob dob dobs* Akela would read to us from *The Jungle Book*, arguably Rudyard Kipling's finest work. Thus I came to learn all about a mongoose called Ricki Ticki Tavi whose life was a constant battle against cobras deep in the Indian jungle. It made a change from Rin Tin Tin. I really enjoyed Cubs and I was worried that if we did move to Sliema as a family I would have to give it all up. I need not have worried.

# 9.

I think it was just after Easter when Dad made an announcement.

'We're moving to Sliema.'

It was not a surprise. All Mum's friends in Dolphin Flats had either moved or were about to move including the Knockolds who were going to North Devon, probably to RAF Chivenor. I sincerely hoped we were not going to Navarino Flats. I didn't like them at all despite the fact that Heather lived there and would be a good friend. They were well back from the water's edge on the other side of a main road. In any case access to the sea there was only via rocks. My concerns were groundless. On our next shopping trip to the NAAFI at Tigne barracks Dad did a slight detour to Hughes Hallet Street to show us where we were going to move to in a couple of weeks. I was not impressed but the place grew on me. Dad parked the Oxford at the end of the street where there seemed to be room for about six cars. We walked the fifty yards to Mirabell House. We were to move into number five on the top floor. All those stairs! Mum was ambivalent.

'At least we have a nice shop opposite.'

She pointed to a general purpose grocers called London Stores. From what was on view through the windows it sold everything we could possibly need from fresh or frozen food to washing powder and beer. Dad would be pleased. And it was called London Stores to remind him of home. More importantly, to me anyway, Mirabell was within a few hundred yards of the famous Tigne Beach Club where Dad's Boys all had affiliated membership. Things were looking up. I was actually looking forward to moving.

Living in Sliema was very different to living at XemXija. It took a bit of getting used to. At the latter I would pop out with my fishing rod and walk a few yards down to the jetty and cast off in the hope of catching a prized black mullet. You could see them but could I ever catch one? It just wasn't that easy at Sliema and fishing from the rocks could be a bit squiffy if there was a sea running.

Sliema was a very built up and populated area. At Mirabell House we were surrounded by streets and buildings although being high up on the third floor we had a great view over rooftops towards the Promenade. We also looked out over the Union Club with its several tennis courts. It always looked half finished to me with building materials and concrete mixers littered everywhere. We only very rarely saw anyone actually playing tennis. Maybe the members spent more time in the cooler bar, particularly in the hot summer months.

We got to know the proprietors of the London Stores quite well – Freddie and Joseph Carmeluzi. Freddie was the older by just a couple of years maybe. It was usually Freddie who served us and we simply called the shop Freddies. We bought our Ollio Sasso there but every so often a vendor using a barrel of olive oil mounted on a donkey drawn cart would shout up the stairwell. *Ollio! Ollio! Ollio!*

It echoed up the stone stairwell for a long time after the last syllable had left his mouth and just to show a little even handedness we would buy some from him. You provided your own bottle or whatever and he simply guessed what to charge you. We usually utilised an empty Gordon's Gin bottle for this purpose and I think the cost was a straight shilling. Weights, measures and EU Rules didn't get a look in then, mate. No way!

Paraffin was also distributed and sold this way. Some people still cooked by paraffin and even some fridges worked with paraffin – don't ask me how as physics wasn't my strongest subject, to put it mildly. We did buy paraffin in the winter for our trusty Aladdin stove which was still going strong. The call up the stairwell this time was *Paraffino! Paraffino!*

The cry was only repeated once, unlike Ollio. More syllables maybe? There's a reason for everything.

I made more friends in Sliema, maybe because more kids lived there. Mum was delighted when an old friend, Peggy Cosstick, arrived from England to live just around the corner. Peggy and Mum had met in the maternity ward of the David Bruce Hospital and her daughter Jean was born four days after me. Jean went to the nearby Tigne Army School. I did not change schools when we moved house, I think because Tigne School was much smaller and probably full to capacity. We still went to St. Andrew's and we caught the school bus, another Army Bedford, on Tower Road right outside the Sliema Branch of Barclays DCO Bank. DCO stood for Dominion, Colonial & Overseas and it retained that name right up until about 1970 when its name was changed to simply Barclays International. When Harold Macmillan's wind of change blew through Africa it didn't do to retain such an Imperial name even if the bank did own half of the continent. A dozen years later I found myself working for that Bank in Yorkshire and by chance one of my managers, John Jackson, had done his banking apprenticeship with DCO in Malawi, then known as Nyasaland. With his colonial and worldly background Mr Jackson never seemed to fit in as a provincial bank manager. Nor did I, come to think of it, not even as a lowly bank clerk.

Jean introduced my sister and me to the potential delights of roller skating. I say potential because one first had to master the skill of staying vertical let alone propelling oneself in a certain direction at a certain rate of knots. The Promenade, outside where the Preluna Hotel is now and the Golden Harvest Café, was flat and even and proved to be a good training ground. The skill was eventually acquired and skates bought with birthday monies sent as postal orders from grandparents, uncles and aunts. The best, and fastest, place to skate was on the Chalet Ghar Id-Dudd. This was a long pier type structure supported by stone pillars jutting out over the sea. It had a tiled floor which is why it was so fast to skate on. You had to go through a gate to get onto the Chalet but I don't recall it ever being locked. It was quite long and in past times had probably been used for music and dancing – not unlike English seaside piers perhaps before corrosion and storms blew most of them down.

Jean was by far the best skater of all of us and her father, Ted, would sometimes take us into the Golden Harvest for a milk-shake afterwards. I often used to see another classmate, Judith Dearden, in the café. I think she must have lived nearby. Judith was quite arty, I recall. We once had to design a logo or mark from our initials and she cleverly used the D on its side with the hump facing upwards, and the J underneath forming an umbrella, the segments of which she painted all different colours. To this day whenever I see the Legal & General insurance logo with its coloured umbrella I think of Judith. Aren't human memories extraordinary?

A couple of days before my ninth birthday on 16<sup>th</sup> July 1962, my Dad took me to buy my first ever wristwatch. We didn't have far to go to *A. Agius – Jewellers since 1938* in Tower Road. The shop was tiny with a frontage of no more than about eight feet but I recall it went back a long way. It had one of those roller shutters that was brought down and secured after hours and during siestas. I was allowed to choose a watch and Dad asked the vendor, presumably Mr Agius, if he stocked a watch called Roamer. He immediately brought forth about six examples made by this company, a very old Swiss manufacturer. Dad wore a Roamer which he bought in Muizenberg, Cape Town, when he was in the Navy almost two decades earlier and which was still serving him well. So I chose one of those with a smart black strap. Mr Agius showed me how to wind it up gently, without too much pressure on the spring. He told me it would last me a lifetime if I looked after it. Unfortunately it didn't get the chance to prove its longevity as it was stolen by a grocery delivery boy in Hong Kong in 1967. I replaced it with another Roamer which lasted me almost another forty years. Mr Agius hadn't been joking had he?

A few doors up from Agius Jewellers was a paper and book shop where we ordered our weekly comics. I took the *Hotspur* (what else for a Spurs fan) and Linda took the *Bunty*. The shop also sold a goodly range of proper fountain pens and I bought one of those with some birthday money along with a bottle of dark blue Quink. My first pen was an Osmiroid. Big mistake. The ink reservoir was filled (or emptied) by extending a little lever that popped out of the side of the pen. To fill it, or refill it, you placed the nib of the pen into the Quink, opened the lever to create a mini vacuum in the reservoir inside the pen, and then slowly replaced the lever to the normal position, sucking up the ink as you did so.

All went well, at first. I took it to school where Mr Manning was encouraging the use of fountain pens as an alternative to pencils. The pen ran out of ink on one occasion and I asked Mr Manning if I could refuel, as it were, from the Quink on his desk. It was just bad luck. His pot was full to capacity and was probably topped up from a bigger container bought in bulk. Dipping the nib end into the ink I gently pulled the little lever and to my horror a stream of bubbles blew blue ink all over his desk top. He was not impressed but at least this was an accident and, unlike the William Tell incident, was not a capital offence. Manning was never short of words and after the ink was mopped up with copious sheets of blotting paper he regained his cool and pronounced to the class: 'Can I recommend the use of Platignum *cartridge* pens as your first step into the world of ink?'

As I mentioned before although he was a strict disciplinarian, Manning was an excellent teacher. It was Army education policy for pupils at their schools overseas to be at least three months ahead of their contemporaries in the UK, to allow for the amount of time some kids had to spend in transit. By the end of that term we were all using proper ink pens; I don't recall ballpoints were in common use by then anyway.

Shortly after my birthday the summer holiday arrived and it was time to make full use of the facilities afforded at Tigne Beach. The word beach was a total misnomer as there was not a grain of sand in sight. On most days just after lunch we would rendezvous with Jean and her mum, Peggy, and walk the several hundred yards to the beach. There was shade and umbrellas for the mums but mostly we just couldn't wait to jump or dive off the rocks or one of several boards into the sea. The water was quite deep and there was little danger of injury from accidentally hitting the bottom. We bought cold drinks and sandwiches from the small café and kiosk on site. No doubt it provided the Club with some income to maintain the facilities and pay the staff. My favourite sandwiches were the local tomato ones. I could, and probably did, eat them every day. I can still taste them now. Unfortunately I did contract 'the Dog' on one occasion which Mum blamed on an unwashed tomato. I think she gave the café owner a piece of her Yorkshire mind in her own charming way. Mum never actually shouted at anybody.

One particular inlet at Tigne was known as the Marsa pool and the water was particularly deep. It needed to be too as the diving board was probably fifteen feet above the surface. I was amazed to see a tiny slip of a girl, probably aged about three or four, jump off the board time after time holding her nose as she did so to stop an ingestion of sea water. She was fearless. She was called Karen Lyall and the daughter of George Lyall, one of Dad's Scottish colleagues at Dingli. Her brother, also called George, became a professional footballer and played for Raith Rovers and Preston North End. Twenty years later whilst working in Scarborough for Barclays I was stunned to discover that the bonny blonde Karen working in the same office was none other than the little mermaid wannabee.

Apart from skating, Jean also rode horses with her friend Ann Tabona who lived nearby. It wasn't long before Peggy persuaded Mum and Dad that maybe Mark and Pinda (her nickname for Linda) might like to learn to ride too. You betcha!

The Riding School was close to the Marsa racetrack. This was not Cheltenham or Ascot, you understand, as the racing was in fact trotting, with a single horse pulling a lightweight, two wheeled carriage upon which was perched the rider, sitting down with reins and whip in hand. It made good spectator sport and competition was fierce amongst individuals and villages that sought the huge silver trophies awarded to the winners. The horses were highly decorated with plumes and finery be-decking their heads and manes.

The riding school was managed by an English lady called Paddy who I think was an Army Officer's wife. She took us in hand on our first day and introduced us to all the horses by name and mane. The smallest was a polo pony stallion called Sandy and he was my favourite, being easy to handle if quite quick sometimes. There was Jebel, a brown Arab mare who was quite docile, and two much larger greys called Tahlet and Cloud. If Sandy was already being ridden by someone else I often chose Tahlet. She was a dappled grey and I did my first canter on her as you could guarantee she would run in a straight line unlike some of the others who seem to have been trained as ice skaters first.

I remember a horse bolting on one occasion with a young girl aboard. It had probably been startled by a lizard or something and within a nanosecond did its best to emulate Larkspur, that year's Derby winner. Paddy and her mount Cloud sprang into action at a gallop, catching up the runaway and grabbing its bridle about two hundred yards later. The lass was in tears but in one piece.

My friend Mike also took up riding at the same school and we often overlapped. I think Cloud was his favourite horse when Paddy wasn't riding her. One Saturday I asked Paddy if I could have a try at polo on the pitch that was contained within the racetrack. My wish was granted and the ball or whatever it's called was duly placed on the ground and a 'bat' placed in my right hand. I led Sandy about twenty yards away and commenced my run up. Swish! Missed. I had another go, in fact a few more goes before I actually made contact but then it didn't go where I thought it was going to go. I decided that polo was not my sport and how stupid to have named it after a mint anyway. Mind you cricket was named after an insect.

There were other sports facilities at the Marsa Club including a cricket pitch and a full sized golf course. Dad acquired several Slazenger woods to accompany his iron blades that he had bought from the pro back in Ganton in Yorkshire. He played a few rounds with a chap called Charlie Patterson, another of his colleagues. After a round one day one of Charlie's sons took his dad's driver from his golf bag together with a tee and a ball. Walking to the edge of the cricket pitch he stuck the tee in the grass, placed the ball on it and practised his swing a few times. The match was still in play so I tried to stop him, but as I did so he opened his shoulders, swung his arms back and the polished head of hardwood hit me right in the forehead. Ouch! A large lump soon appeared. Charlie heard the commotion and was furious with his son. It put me off ever trying to play golf for about a decade.

There was some lighter entertainment that afternoon as about tea time a lone Canberra bomber sporting RAF markings zoomed quite low over the cricket pitch several times. There wasn't much grass in Malta and the island's sole dairy herd of Ayrshires used to graze all over the golf course as it was usually well irrigated I recall. The plane must have scared the shit out of the cows. Maybe that was the idea: cheap fertiliser perhaps.The Army was omnipresent but RAF activity was never far away too as Malta's air space is small as the Luftwaffe and Italian Air Force will gladly confirm. Apart from the Canberras based at Luqa there were the previously mentioned Shacks based at Ta'Qali and regular deployments of other squadrons from the UK. You usually heard them before you saw them. I remember one day my dad urging me to join him on the roof of Mirabell House. In the sky to the southeast and not very far away a flight of Avro Vulcan bombers were making their descent into Luqa. There were probably about eight of them in line astern. Painted all white they shone in the sun like lasers as we gazed beyond Sliema Creek towards Valletta.

Looking at a map today they were obviously landing on the runway whose approach was from the northeast over the Three Cities. The noise of a lone Vulcan is never to be forgotten. Now try to imagine eight of them.

There was a third air base at Hal Far in the extreme southeast of the island and it was used jointly between the RAF and the Fleet Air Arm with carrier based planes using the air base when the carriers themselves were moored in Grand Harbour. It was standard practice to disembark the air wing when in port if possible but I do remember some exercises taking place with jets being catapulted off stationary carrier decks in Grand Harbour which would then fly round to Hal Far and land.

The Royal Navy belonged to Malta and vice versa. It was, after all, Lord High Admiral Nelson's Fleet that had routed and removed the French from the island in 1800. Their occupation had lasted only two years, but the British would last almost two centuries. Had Nelson failed would we be seeing today Kronenbourg instead of Hop Leaf and frogs' legs instead of rabbit?

The views from our roof, as I mentioned, were spectacular. At any given time there were usually three or four destroyers moored in Sliema Creek, often American ones too which sported a darker grey than Royal Navy ships and made them easy to distinguish. Their pennant numbers were also painted in white, not black, nearer to the bow and had a shadow in black to accentuate the numbering. Dad bought a small but very effective pair of Japanese binoculars and we spent many hours shipspotting from the roof. One of our destroyers sported the number D77 and Dad used to call it HMS *Sunset Strip*. It was decades before I discovered that its real name was *Trafalgar*. Nelson would have surely turned in his St. Paul's Cathedral grave if he had heard Dad.

# 10.

Apart from the ferries from Naples to Ischia and Capri the year before I had still not been on board a proper ship. Dad's first ship had been the battleship *Resolution*, mine was the *Skylark* in Peasholm Park. I had come close to being invited onto a large ship when living at XemXija. Vaughan Gordon had an uncle, I think his mother's brother, who was serving on the heavy cruiser HMS *Lion* which was due to visit Valletta soon and a tour of the ship would be arranged. Sadly it didn't happen. Maybe the *Lion* didn't get to Malta after all.

In May 1962 I finally got my wish. A colleague of Dad's called George Winpenny asked Dad if I would like to accompany him and his two sons on a visit to an American aircraft carrier which was on a goodwill visit to Malta as part of a NATO deployment. You bet! I was so excited. On the appointed day, a Saturday, we went in the Winpenny's family car to Valletta and parked somewhere below the Barrakka Gardens which overlook Grand Harbour. Out there in the middle close to Fort St. Angelo was the biggest ship I had ever seen. It was the USS *Shangri-La,* an Essex Class carrier of the United States Sixth Fleet. She looked absolutely magnificent and I couldn't wait to get on board. There was quite a queue of people at the jetty where liberty boats from the carrier were ferrying visitors to and fro.

We had a fantastic time. Climbing up the long ladder from a sort of floating platform was an adventure in itself. The crew were all dressed in tropical whites with hats at a jaunty angle and to me they all looked like Popeye. On boarding we were all handed a blue and white leaflet entitled *Welcome Aboard the USS Shangri-La*. I still have my copy today over half a century later. We spent about two hours aboard and were magnificently looked after by our American hosts. The immense flight deck was where it all happened of course and for me the highlight was climbing up an access ladder and actually sitting in the cockpit of a fighter jet. I think it was a Voodoo, but I wouldn't put money on it.

*Now don't you guys touch anything, ye'all. Or ye'all be getting airborne!*

So we didn't. We just imagined being blasted off the sharp end by the steam catapult. We were fed chocolate cake, cookies and popcorn until it came out of our ears. Another memorable moment was standing in a row as though we were all on parade on the deck lift. A warning klaxon was sounded and the lift dropped down quickly to the hangar deck below. I had never seen so many planes in my life and they were all crammed in so tight you wondered how they got them all in and out. When it was time to leave they piped us off with a bosun's whistle. It truly was a day to remember.

US warships were frequent visitors to Malta and I distinctly remember the raked bows of the *Coontz* Class destroyers moored in Sliema Creek. The US Navy usually maintained two carriers in the Mediterranean and at that time the *Shangri-La's* sister was the *Kitty Hawk*. Over a decade later, in Hong Kong, I would befriend a US Navy Commander called Gordon Bedford who was a Supply

Officer on the *Kitty Hawk* and we exchanged tales of his own visit to Malta.

Perhaps, though, the USN's most important role within Maltese waters was in December 1989 when the cruiser USS *Belknap*, acting in her capacity as flagship of the Sixth Fleet, hosted the Malta summit between President George H W Bush and the Soviet Leader, Mikhail Gorbachev. It formally marked the end of the Cold War and the popular press dubbed it *from Yalta to Malta* in reference to the Yalta Conference in 1945 that had agreed European boundaries at the end of the Second World War. The *Belknap* and the Soviet cruiser *Slava* were anchored in Marsaxlokk Bay for the occasion which was bedevilled by bad weather. Nevertheless it put Malta on the international map for all the right reasons.

I was still able to go to Cubs every Tuesday because the Army laid on transport for all of us who lived in Sliema and Paceville. This time it wasn't the familiar bus, though, it was a three ton Bedford truck. The pick-ups started at Tigne Barracks, only five minutes from Mirabell. I would walk straight past the guardhouse, giving any occupant who saw me a mock salute, and carry on, usually sucking an iced lolly that I had bought at a newsagents and general store called, appropriately, the *Gunners Rest*. I never had to wait for the truck's driver who was already at the wheel and ready to go. He would always give a friendly wave and gesture for me to jump straight into the back to sit which was easier said than done. It was quite a high climb over the tailgate before sitting on one of the rock hard metal bench seats.

The drivers were all from the Argyll and Sutherland Highlanders who were based at Tigne for years. You couldn't miss them with their tartan keppies and the black tassel at the back falling down their sunburned necks. We stopped at several points en route including outside the chapel opposite Dick's Bar in Spinola. A lad called Peter Robb always got on here and by the time we got to the scout hut we were probably about ten strong. The same driver usually took us back home in the opposite direction two hours later. I was always first on and last off but on the way home he would drop me at the end of Hughes Hallet Street to save me the last few hundred yards' walk. That was especially appreciated in the summer when our khaki shirts would be dripping wet with perspiration. Four years later I passed through Aden on a ship bound for Hong Kong. Aden was in civil and military turmoil as terrorists tried to bomb their way into power. We were civilian passengers in a very dangerous place so the Argylls, who had been transferred to Aden from Malta, assigned a platoon to look after us. I wondered at the time if any of them had been the driver of the truck that took me to Cubs. You just never know do you?

It was to the Gunners Rest that I walked most afternoons to buy the *Daily Express* for Dad. After being printed in Fleet Street supplies of English papers were driven to Heathrow or Gatwick and then flown out to Gibraltar, Malta, Libya and Cyprus. I think the *Express* cost five pence in old money. Dad would give me a tanner (sixpence) and often let me buy a big gob-stopper with the penny change. Sometimes the papers were late and you had to go back later. Headwinds over the Tyrolean Sea maybe? The older turbo-props couldn't fly as high as modern jets and were often affected by bad weather conditions. A delay of ten minutes today probably equated to a couple of hours back in the early sixties.

Dad just had to have his *Express* every day. Today we would call him a news junkie or something equally unflattering but what is wrong with wanting news from home? There were no multi-channel TVs or online papers in those days. We did have a good wireless, though, and even a TV, courtesy of Rediffusion, a British company that pioneered many aspects of communications, radio and electronics. In its day the company was a world leader.

We had just one television channel. Can you imagine that? TV had been going for a good five years in the UK but it had taken a while to catch up in Malta. It was cable, and it came from studios at a place called Gwardamanga (*Guard a Manger* was the nearest we got to pronouncing it correctly). I think the main radio stations were based there too judging from the number of huge aerials reaching skywards from several buildings. The only time I ever remember going to Gwardamanga was to do my House Orderly proficiency test at a posh lady's house. She was obviously something to do with the Scout movement and was the test examiner. I had to hoover the whole house, clean and cook a light meal which I remember very well: it was fried bacon, eggs and tomatoes, rounded off with a pot of tea and bread and butter. Much to my surprise I was then invited to eat it. I only made one mistake and that was forgetting to take the butter from the fridge long before I needed to spread it. It was like spreading concrete. No matter, I passed. Mum said I would. I had practised cracking eggs into a pan without breaking the yolks for weeks. Mike belonged to the Savoy Branch of the Cubs but I'll bet you he never passed the House Orderly badge. To this day he can't even make an egg sandwich.

Anyway, I digress, as I am apt to do as you will have noticed if you've read this far. The programmes on TV were grim. We had a mixture of English, American and Australian offerings including Leave it to Beaver, Mr Ed (the talking horse), Ten Town and the Flying Doctor. I am sure it was the last two that ignited my interest in Australia at such a young age. It was odd that Australian programmes should feature on TV on a small island eight thousand miles away from the sub-continent. They were perhaps amongst the first indications, to me at least, of the very strong links between Malta and Australia. Like the links between the UK and Australia they are written in blood and will never go away. As for adult viewing, I think I'm right in saying that *77 Sunset Strip*, starring Efrem Zimbalist Jr, was new to the screen and compulsive viewing for all mums at least.

Dad was more of a radio man, as you might expect, and we had a wireless in the kitchen, the dining room and the lounge. If he wasn't at work we had to endure the seven o'clock ritual of the News from the BBC World Service. Firstly you got the opening bars of *Lillibullero*, then Big Ben and then: *This is London, the world news read by Philip Treleaven* or whoever.

It was proper news then too from London and around the world, not the sanctimonious claptrap churned out now by left wing *Guardian* readers living like parasites on the licence fee payers' money. It was followed by *News about Britain* which might include news of sporting events such as the Boat Race, the Ashes Test, or the Queen opening a new hospital, theatre or whatever. In those days you never felt far from home if you listened to the BBC. Today it's like listening to another planet. Zog maybe?

Television apart, one of the advantages of living in town, as it were, was the number of cinemas within easy reach. I took great advantage of this. I saw the *Alamo* and *Fantasia* at the Alhambra, *Journey to the Centre of the Earth* at the Majestic and, most memorably of all, *Ben Hur* in Valletta, I think at the Capital. On Mike's tenth birthday in the November a load of us went to see Norman Wisdom in *The*

*Girl on the Boat,* also in Valletta. For some reason known only to ourselves we decided to walk back to his flat in Rudolf Street and his mum Beryl was not pleased as we were all late for the birthday tea she had laid on for us. Maybe we wanted to save the bus fares, I can't remember. It was also Beryl's birthday and Mum had reminded me to wish her a happy birthday too.

Cinemas apart, from time to time we were often regally entertained, movie wise, by a colleague of Dad's called Norman Fox. Norman was a Brummie and one of his passions in life, apart from food and wine, was collecting old black and white movies starring the likes of Charlie Chaplin, Laurel and Hardy and the Keystone Cops. On warm evenings (which in Malta was nearly every evening) he would set up his projector, a Eumig, and project the films onto the white wall without requiring a screen. Norman and his wife Georgette, who was originally from the Lebanon, had a son, Mike, a year younger than me and twin girls, Ruth and Marianne, just a few years younger still.

Other kids would be invited round, snacks and Cokes distributed, and we would howl our heads off. Until the film broke, which was frequent. Or was it an excuse for Norman and Dad to top their glasses up. Looking back now, as an adult, the tape seemed to break awfully frequently. Splicing the film back together again took about five minutes.

The Foxes lived in an area called The Gardens on slightly higher ground to the northwest of Spinola. It was quite a popular area for expats and our headmaster, Mr Ozouf, lived there too. No official Army car and driver for him. He got on the school bus about eight o'clock just like the rest of us. The Foxes' block of flats was surrounded by much open ground and I remember a market garden nearby growing lots of melons which you could buy via an honesty box.

Apart from showing his children's films Norman also had his own cine camera. Dad got bitten by the bug too and he bought his own Super 8mm triple lensed Crown Cronica camera. And so began Dad's three year career as a moviemaker. Steven Spielberg was only eighteen at the time but he need not have worried too much at the coming competition from my dad. He soon got the hang of it, well sort of. We had lots of dummy runs and he practised using the three available lenses – standard, wide angle and telephoto. Some of the earlier attempts were of me and Linda on horseback at the Marsa. However I think that by the time the correct telephoto lens had been selected we looked like outlaws escaping into the distance. *Bonanza* it was not to be.

He did take some good shots of us diving into the sea which when played backwards on the projector showed us coming out of the sea, feet first, and returning back to the diving board. Consideration was given to buying Granny and Grandad a projector in England and posting them some of our home-made films. Wisely, this was not pursued and we stuck to tape recordings. Grandad would not have coped with a broken tape, splicing and *lights on/lights off please*.

There was one major drawback to this type of camera. When the film ran out after about ten minutes' filming you had to open the camera and turn the tape over to double the running time. This you had to do in the dark lest your forthcoming Oscar winner be exposed to light and ruined. Darkness is not a commodity in plentiful supply in sun drenched Malta. The other potential hazard was that of turning over the tape twice, hence doubly exposing the first side of the film. This happened on several occasions which are almost too embarrassing to mention. On the way home the following year we ended up with some trolleybuses in Naples seemingly going up the river under the Ponte Veccio in Florence and in 1966 some camels by the Suez Canal walking through Uncle George's dahlias.

Home movies have come a long way since then and nowadays a camcorder won't allow you to make that sort of error. One particular piece of action though that Dad did make an excellent job of was lengthy footage of a small freighter attempting to enter Grand Harbour. It was mid-winter and a horrendous sea was running from the northeast. There is a long harbour mole at the northern side of the entrance to Grand Harbour and this necessitates an approach around it followed by a sharpish turn to port to curve around the southern harbour mole. Whilst this normally presents no difficulty to a pilot or experienced helmsman, in those sea conditions it looked hazardous. The vessel made three failed approaches turning hard a-starboard at the last possible moment. Large crowds gathered to watch. On the fourth attempt the Captain got it right and the crowd that had gathered to watch cheered and clapped. Maybe some of those watching had also clapped the *Ohio* into safety too two decades earlier.

We did wonder why the ship didn't just ride out the storm at sea. Maybe it was low on fuel, you just never know. It was yet another example of the sanctuary that Grand Harbour could provide whether you were a tanker barely afloat or a small freighter seeking calm waters. We witnessed another example of this when fire broke out on the shiny new passenger liner *Canberra* on its way from England to Australia. Half-way through the Mediterranean and en route to the Suez Canal a serious fire had seriously disabled the vessel and forcd her to take refuge in Grand Harbour. Hundreds of emigrating 'ten pound Poms' were taken off and flown onwards in chartered aircraft. The vessel was 'made good' but I wonder how many Maltese took the opportunity to join the partly-emptied accommodation and emigrate themselves to the Lucky Country.

Dad stunned us all one day when out of the blue he suddenly announced that he intended to photograph every church and chapel in Malta. Dear God, what was all this in aid of? He wasn't joking, either. I believe there were over four hundred of them. Looking back I attribute it to the conscience of a lapsed Catholic. Brought up in a large North London Catholic family of Italian, Flemish and Irish make-up I think he probably lapsed when he joined the Navy, if not straight away, then when the second torpedo slammed into the lower mess decks of the *Resolution,* killing some shipmates. I think he always felt a bit Catholic, though, despite marrying my Protestant mother whose closest religious affectations were probably collecting the fruit and veg for the village church's harvest festival. Farmers' daughters are like that.

Anyway, whatever the reason, the next six months were different to say the least. Detailed cartographic maps were acquired. Ecclesiastical maps were purloined from God knows where and every weekend brought forth a new destination, usually in the middle of nowhere, for the Oxford to reach. Actually I quite enjoyed the geographical bit and it made me a good map reader for life. These vehicular and spiritual journeys where the only times I sat in the front of the Oxford, folded maps on my lap, as I directed Dad to port or starboard all over the island. Maybe I should have become a navigating officer. Or maybe I had been one in a previous life? It sure felt like it.

One particular chapel, which can't have measured more than twelve feet square, was actually in the middle of a field full of potatoes and the crop was being harvested that day and about a dozen children were gathering up the spuds into boxes of every size you could imagine. Having taken two shots of the chapel from slightly different angles Dad returned to the car, opened the boot and pulled out a yellow plastic shopping basket and asked the children to fill it for him.

And so it went on. And on. I think by about Easter he was done.

It was just as well Gozo wasn't on the menu as well as we were due to leave for England the following year. We did manage one single trip to Gozo though, courtesy of Norman Fox who had been before and would act as our guide. I recall he sat in the front with Dad as we drove to Marfa, then the ferry terminal on the northern tip of the island. The ferry was quite small and carried only passengers as I recall. It took about half-an-hour to get there and I seem to remember we hired two cars with drivers.

We had a grand tour of most of Gozo, walked up the Citadel in Victoria, commonly known as Rabat and stopped for a seafood lunch in Marsalforn on the north coast. Thankfully we were spared any churches, chapels or pre-Christian ruins on this occasion. When we got back to the 'Gardens' Georgette had prepared a lovely tea for us. By the day's end I think I had reached the conclusion that Gozo was an 'adult' destination.

We had more visitors from the UK in the shape of Dad's eldest brother John and his son Ivor. Uncle John had a small factory in Enfield, Middlesex, that manufactured belts for ladies' outfits. His wife Winnifred, Aunty Winn to me, did not come with them. It was only a small factory and maybe she was holding the fort. Uncle John was a nice man; he had a rich voice that carried a long way and you felt compelled to listen to him whatever he was talking about.

He used to walk down to the Gunners Rest with me most afternoons and I remember he was most displeased to find that it was the *Express*, the *Mail* or sod all. His favourite *Telegraph* of which he was an avid reader for fifty years was unavailable. Perhaps being a very large and heavy broadsheet it was just uneconomic to send it to Malta by air. The Gunners Rest also sold war comics and he almost always bought me one: they were a shilling each, a lot of money in those days. They also sold Airfix aeroplane models and I remember he bought me a Spitfire. Dorniers, Heinkels and Aermacchi dive bombers were also on display but Maltese folk have long memories and German and Italian models sold very slowly, unlike Spitfires, Hurricanes and Mosquitoes that sold like hot cakes whenever a new delivery came in from England. That's Malta for you, always loyal.

Malta's famous buses could take you to just about any part of the island and I offered to take Ivor anywhere he wanted to go. The problem was that Ivor didn't like buses. At thirteen Ivor was four years older than me and had already assumed, in his mind, adult status. He preferred to wear long trousers instead of shorts despite the heat and on one evening looked quite absurd sporting a pair of tartan trews. He looked a total twerp. Mum and Dad, together with Moss and Joyce, were taking Uncle John to their favourite restaurant in Sliema called the City Gem in Prince of Wales Road. Ivor just assumed that he was invited too. Dad cut him down to size sharply. 'It's adults only tonight, Ivor. You can have some Coke on the balcony with Mark and Linda.' Ivor was furious and sulked for the next twenty-four hours.

He never did get to the City Gem but to be honest neither did I. I walked past it many times as it was the shortest route whenever I walked to see Mike at the other end of Rudolf Street. The route also took me past Holy Trinity Church where I was Christened. We took Uncle John and Ivor to meet the Azzopardis. The old man was pleased to meet Dad's brother and they had short conversations via the interpreting skills of one of the daughters. He gave Uncle John a gift of several quails he had recently shot. With the exception of Canberras and Vickers Viscounts anything that moved through Maltese airspace was 'fair game' at certain times of the year. It is something that does not endear Malta to the rest of the world. I can't remember whether we actually ate them or not. As a farmer's daughter Mum might well have plucked and roasted them.

A day on Little Armier Beach was a day to remember for Uncle John but for all the wrong reasons. He got his feet badly sunburnt. Seeking some shade in our beach tent he had unfortunately taken forty winks and left his two milky white North London feet sticking outside. Malta's July sun is unforgiving and he awoke with feet the colour of boiled lobsters. He was in pain for days and unable to wear sandals, let alone shoes.

Uncle John stayed with us two weeks but somehow it was decided that Ivor would stay on another two weeks. The tartan trews never reappeared. Shorts and flip flops were purchased inexpensively and he joined in with me and my local friends when we went to Tigne Beach or went fishing. In Sliema my favourite place to fish was in Sliema Creek not far from the ferry terminal to Valletta. Although quite a few motor boats and yachts used to tie up there you could always find room to cast out. We shared my four section pole from Bur-Marrad and I think Ivor was quite enthused as time went by. He was very clean cut and I don't think that putting worms on hooks down on the River Lee near Edmonton was quite his scene. As youngsters our fathers had fished and swum there for years. When his extra two weeks were over we took him to the airport for his flight to London where his dad was going to meet him. It would be just over a year before we saw him again.

# 11.

Christmas in 1962 was, as usual, sunny and mild. Ted Cosstick took Jean, Linda and myself to see *Cinderella,* pantomime but I cannot for the life of me remember exactly where. I know it was quite a way in his Ford Classic to get there wherever it was. I think it might have been in a Forces Theatre somewhere. On Christmas Day itself we actually went roller skating on the Promenade before our turkey lunch, again provided by the Azzopardi family.

A few months earlier they had moved out of the cave into a stone house they had built adjacent to the nearest road. They had proudly shown us around the house which this time did have electricity, I think. When Dad and I had called to collect the turkey Mr Azzopardi was ploughing a nearby field with a donkey. He gestured for me to have a go. I was game for it and just for once I wished that Dad had brought his cine camera. I made clicking noises and jangled the reins expecting to be pulled into action at about three knots. Big problem: the donkey refused to budge. The old boy shouted something loud in Maltese to it, *Ejja imxi!* (*Imshee*) or something like that and whoosh! The beast set off at about five knots and almost pulled me over. So ended my first (and last) attempt at ploughing, by animal or machine. I'm sure the family uses petrol powered rotovators today. I sure hope so for their sake. There were so many stones in the field that Fred Flintstone and Barney Rubble would have felt quite at home. Sadly the TV series that parodied the American way of life hadn't yet reached Malta.

By now I was in Class 3A and thoughts started to turn towards our next school which would be in England. Our new form teacher was a Mr Lawes. He was very friendly and after Manning was a welcome change. Looking back, though, I have to say he was not as good a teacher as Manning and there is no doubt that time was lost and very little progress made, especially in arithmetic. We just seemed to go over old ground all the time. Lawes was leaving in the summer, as were many of us, and no doubt he was being posted to another Forces school which might have been in Germany.

When we did eventually get back to Scarborough, I found myself three months behind my new classmates and my new teacher and headmaster said it would be touch and go whether I could catch up in time to pass my Eleven Plus exam the following year. The same thing happened to Mike in Winchester who had 'all on'to catch up too. Fortunately we both just managed to pass which would lead to us being classmates again three years later. Our experience was not typical of Army schools which, as mentioned, tried to keep their pupils three months ahead, not three months behind.

But back to Malta: I can't remember exactly when, but I think about February, Dad received a telegram about Grandpa from his eldest sister, Eva. It read something like: *Dad seriously ill stop ring John stop Eva.*

As telegrams go, it was about as short as you can get. You paid by the word but I think the 'stops' were free. It was delivered to Mirabell by an employee of Cable and Wireless riding a bright red motorbike.

Dad was obviously worried but knew that sister Eva was prone to panic about these things. We didn't have a telephone so we jumped into the Oxford and drove to Cable and Wireless in Paceville. You couldn't miss it as it was sited in rough ground and surrounded by tall radio masts. Dad asked to book a call to England. You had to give them the number you wanted to ring, pay in advance, get in a queue and wait. It was ages before a member of staff bawled through a small hatch into the waiting room. *Mr Hal And... booth number two!* Dad jumped in and shut the door behind him. There was only room for one person. You had three minutes as your allotted time and irritating beeps sounded to give you notice that you had ten seconds left. Dad duly emerged looking less cheerful that usual.

'It's not good I'm afraid, Boy. Pop is in a bad way and heading for a Naval hospital for surgery.'

Pop was a vet of just about every Naval campaign and battle you could imagine: China Station, Gallipoli, Jutland, the Zeebrugge Raid. You name it. Dad was thinking on his feet and quickly came up with an idea. A couple of hundred yards away lived a colleague, one Stan Wilkinson, his wife Nan and their daughter Margaret. They were from North Shields and spoke, to me at least, with the same unintelligible twang as the Gordons from my days in XemXija. They were lovely folk and More Grit, as they called their brunette daughter was at school with Linda. Stan was going on shift at Dingli within a very short time and would speak to the welfare officer who would send proper signals to his opposite numbers in London. There would be no 'stop' to finish with. It would read *message ends*. All Admiralty signals finished that way.

Things happened very quickly after that. Dad was on a plane back to London within twenty-four hours as the worst was feared. Happily it didn't happen. Pop lived to fight another day and was advised to cut down on his rum ration, as it were.

When Dad returned to Malta about a week later he complained that he had flown into the tail end of the coldest winter in England for years. He had however managed to take in a Spurs home game at White Hart Lane and he told me that their new striker recently signed from AC Milan was just magic. His name was Jimmy Greaves. He also took the opportunity to invest the sum of fifty pounds in the shares of a new company called Enfield Electronics after purely by chance reading a story in the *Edmonton Herald*. That company name eventually disappeared but history recorded them as the original inventors of the aeroplane Black Box which is at the heart of every accident investigation.

Shortly after Easter came more visitors from home. This time it was my mum's brother Bert, his wife Alice and their son David who was only about five years old. I think it was their first overseas holiday and they enjoyed every moment of it. In fact we all did. The weather was kind and we drove all over the island. On several occasions when Dad was at work he shared a lift to Dingli with a colleague so that Uncle Bert could drive the Oxford. I think he had one of his own back in Stafford where he worked for English Electric as a switchgear designer so it was quite easy for him. By coincidence they lived at 302 Oxford Gardens in Stafford, an address that was committed to memory for the umpteen thank you letters I wrote following generous postal orders at Christmas and birthdays. We drove all over the island, getting lost many times without Dad as navigator and pilot.

One day we visited Peter the Potter who turned out dishes, bowls, vases and even ashtrays from his spinning wheel. I think it was operated by a foot powered treadle as I don't recall a donkey being involved this time. I know we bought Dad an ashtray for a laugh, as if he didn't have enough of them already. Sorry to say I cannot for the life of me remember whereabouts on the island Peter the Potter was. Will somebody reading this enlighten me please? They stayed with us for two weeks and we were all very sorry when it was time to say goodbye. Linda and I had our goodbye hugs and kisses as we went to bed one night as their flight left at silly o'clock in the morning and I think Dad took them to Luqa Airport in the early hours.

A really weird thing happened a few months before we left Malta. Dad and I drove into Valletta one Saturday morning. For once it was raining, an omen perhaps. I wondered where on earth we were going. Parking the Oxford near the Great Ditch we walked over the moat past the omni-present begging nuns and walked straight down Kingsway, as it was then called. After a few hundred yards we turned left into, of all things, a music shop. Or more accurately a musical instrument shop. It was dark and forbidding and it gave me the creeps. After a couple of minutes a dark haired, extremely well dressed gentleman came from a room behind and into the main shop area. The conversation between my dad and the as yet unknown (to me) gentleman went something like this.

'Ah good morning, Professor Vallente.' They shook hands.

'Buongiorno, Victor. And this is Marco...'

'Yes, this my son Mark who dearly wishes to learn to play the violin.'

What the heck was all this about?

'Oh no I don't!'

I turned and ran out of the shop. I was horrified. I didn't like violins. To me they sounded like creaking garden gates that need a good squirt of oil. Within minutes we were back in the Oxford and the only words Dad spoke all the way home were: 'I am so embarrassed. You have just turned down the offer to be taught by one of the world's most eminent violinists.'

He should at least have asked me first. I was in no way musically inclined, at least from a playing point of view. I think Mum had the last word on the subject:

'What on earth was your father thinking about?'

I guess it was Italian genes and all that. Certainly it was never mentioned again. Not ever. Very odd.

# 12.

The end of our three year tour was in sight. Whilst I was going to be sorry to leave 'my island', which by now was my first home, it would be great to see my grandparents again. I missed them very much. It would be good to see Dad's parents too in London before we journeyed north to Yorkshire. The summer term at St. Andrew's just whizzed by. There was nothing really memorable to report. We had more outdoor picture shows at the Foxes' house. Moss, Joyce and Susan had already left and were already back home in Scarborough. Granny's last tape confirmed this. 'Your Dad has just taken two nice lettuces down to Joyce... it won't be long before you're all home eating nice English food too.'

I'd grown rather used to spaghetti, timpana, swordfish, lampuki, plum tomatoes and Ollio and the thought of steak and kidney pie, smelly cabbage and mashed potato was already sounding simply awful. I wouldn't be getting any wine, either, with or without water. Still, with a bit of luck, we'd be back here in another three years time and I could go to the senior school Tal Handaq which was administered by the Navy and not by boot crunching squaddies. That was the hope anyway. Mark the eternal optimist.

As per usual, Dad's official announcements were reserved for the tea table.

'We're going home by sea, train and sea. We leave here on the *Citta di Tunisi* on Saturday 10th August. The boat takes us to Naples where we get off. We spend three days there then go by train to Rome where we spend another three days. Then we go by train to Turin for two days then a train to Paris for two days then a final French train to Calais. From there we get a boat to Dover in Kent and then a train to London. Any questions?'

The only question I wanted to ask was *Do we really have to go back to England?* but I thought better of it. We had to go and that was it. I started to give things away that I didn't want to take home. I gave my model planes to Brian and my fishing rod to a chap called Michael O'Hara who was a year above me at school. His father was an Army Sergeant who had recently arrived from Episcopi in Cyprus. We had fished regularly in Sliema Creek and further round the headland at Dragut Point which was named after an Ottoman Admiral who fought against Malta in the Great Siege. That was unusual in Malta. Muslim names were usually cast into Hell not remembered by naming places after them.

We had some light relief in early May when we watched the FA Cup Final 'live' at the private house of the family that owned the Plevna Hotel just around the corner. I think his name was Gordon Tabona. You could only see the match via Italian television signals boosted via Sicily which I suppose was a change from dive bombers. Manchester United beat Leicester City 3-1. At half time we all piled across the road to the hotel itself for tea, cakes and sandwiches. I seem to remember a lot of cigarette smoke in the dining room too.

School broke up for the summer a few days after my tenth birthday on July 16th. It was awful saying goodbye to people you would probably never see again. Caroline, Heather, Evelyn, Judith, Monica – and that was just the girls. I shook hands with Mr Lawes, said my goodbyes to Reginald, Vaughan and Geoffrey and got on the school bus home. A chapter of my little life had ended. I would see Mike and Brian again before we left Malta and Mick Church was also heading for Scarborough so I would see him before too long. I also said goodbye to the nice Mr Ozouf. as his office was the last door on the right as you went out to the buses. Such a nice man. The bus ride home to Sliema was a blur.

Slowly we started to pack things for the journey home. I was perplexed when our wooden canteen of Sheffield cutlery was not placed on the 'pack manifest' and a few other things too. I think we had the Oxford until about two days before we actually left and we sold it to a Navy dentist who worked on Manoel Island. A shiny new black Oxford with chrome bumpers was waiting for us back in Hull to where it had been shipped.

A few days before we left we had our last outing and drive, to the Azzopardis, of course. We said our goodbyes with many tears and we gave them the rug from our dining room and the Aladdin paraffin stove to keep the winter chill at bay. When Mum handed over our canteen of Sheffield cutlery you would have thought we had given them the Crown Jewels. I'll bet you some members of the family are still using the knives and forks somewhere.

Three days before we sailed we moved into an annex of the Plevna Hotel called 'Cathay.' Why it was named after the ancient name for China I do not know. Malta had nothing to do with China, not yet anyway. On the Friday, the day before excommunication, damnation and departure, I took my last walk down Tigne Street to buy my last *Daily Express*. To this day I can still remember the headline: *MAIL TRAIN HIJACKED: MILLIONS MISSING.*

It was the first report in the national press of what was to become known as the Great Train Robbery and its ramifications are almost as newsworthy fifty years later as they were then. The names of Ronnie Biggs, the main criminal behind the audacious plot, and Jack Slipper, the Scotland Yard investigating officer who arrested him in Brazil many years later, are perhaps more familiar today, thanks to the internet, than they were in 1963.

Unusually for me I do not remember what we ate for our 'last supper' at the Plevna Hotel. I felt like a condemned man but at least he would have been able to choose what he had for his last meal.

The *City of Tunis* slipped her moorings in Grand Harbour about noon the following day and I watched from the stern as the floating rock of Malta, my island, disappeared into the heat haze.

# PART 2

OK that's the historical memoirs over with. Like a Time Lord I have now leapt forward an amazing forty- five years. To parody Neil Armstrong......that's one giant leap...... for a ten year old. I had not been to, seen, from land, sea or air, the Island of Malta for four- and- a-half decades. Since leaving I had been around the world by sea on no less than three different vessels, flown to the Middle East many times, the Far East even more times and North America once. I had visited Belgium no less than forty times and to say I was well travelled would have been an understatement. Earlier that year I had been to Australia for the first time which satisfied a long held ambition. But my planned return to Malta would, I hope, eclipse them all. I just couldn't wait to step off that plane at Luqa.

The duck egg blue Thomson Airways Boeing 737 made its approach from the northwest. I could just make out the lights of Gozo as we descended into Maltese airspace. It was late evening and dark but as we got lower I could make out XemXija then Mosta Dome. We touched down and taxied to the terminal. It was early summer and the air was warm. I walked out onto the steps that ground crew had pushed towards the forward door and took a deep breath. Mediterranean air has a scent all of its own, particularly at night. It reminded me of Cyprus which had been a regular stopping off point for me when I worked in Saudi Arabia.

As I stepped off the last step onto the tarmac I muttered to myself: *I'm back. I'm finally back.*

I was tempted to kiss the ground but only Popes do that. I was childishly happy. My travelling companion, Terry McMahon, who was a former colleague of Dad's, was just a few paces behind me. He probably couldn't wait for a fag but would have to wait until we had claimed baggage and cleared Immigration. It didn't take long as the airport was fairly quiet at this time of night. In fact clearing Immigration was a two second formality as the Officer gave only a cursory glance at our maroon EU passports. Malta had been a member of the European Union for just over three years and, unlike the UK, had given up its own currency, the Maltese lira, and joined in with a dozen other nations to adopt the euro. The cynic that I am dubs them IBVs (International Booze Vouchers). We were soon out into the foyer and looking for our transfer notice to the hotel in Sliema. We were directed to a line of waiting coaches all of which appeared to be empty. I spoke to a chap who I thought might be a driver and made enquiries.

'Yes, Plaza Hotel Sliema. The coach at the end.'

He didn't say which end so we just got on the first one. We could not believe it but the coach was built by Plaxton's, a Scarborough company about a mile from where we both lived. It looked like a late seventies coach to me: it even had metal ashtrays on the back of every seat. Terry was so pleased.

'Well if they've got ashtrays, Boy, that must mean you can smoke.'

So he did. Sadly Dad had passed away two years before so Terry had taken to calling me 'Boy' just as my Dad had done for decades. That was fine by me. A few other passengers boarded too and it was probably getting on for midnight by the time we pulled out of the coach park and headed for the nearest hotel drop-off. I tried to get my bearings but after forty-five years and in the dark this was not easy. I soon saw some signs for Marsa, where I had learnt to ride, and then a large crane, so I knew we were near Marsa Dock, the most inland of Grand Harbour's many inlets. I was starting to feel at home already.

About twenty minutes later after the first drop-off not far from Manoel Island I did get all my bearings firmly fixed. Sliema Creek was on the right as we headed towards Tower Road. We turned left up Tower Hill, as we called it, past Victor's Pharmacy (Dad always called it *his* chemists) and I was transfixed as we past Agius Jewellers where Dad had bought me my first watch in 1962 and then a few doors further up the newsagents where I used to collect *Hotspur* every week. I simply could not believe it. They were still there. Was I in a bus or a time capsule?

Within minutes we had travelled the length of Tower Road and past several landmarks which I recognised. I searched to my right to spot the Chalet Ghar Id Dudd but I failed to see it in the dark. It was probably about one in the morning and what struck me was how many people were still walking about. We checked into the Plaza Hotel and went to our large studio style room which faced the rear of the hotel and looked out over hundreds of roofs. We slept well.

Breakfast was on the sixth floor in a large dining room that was heaving with people. It was run buffet style with hot servers dispensing the usual fare of English breakfast including the most divine fried bread. It felt a bit like a NAAFI again as we queued for everything then grabbed a window table. This was going to be my first view of Malta in daylight since August 1963 and I wanted to take it in and enjoy the moment. I gazed northwards towards the casino at Dragonara and my eyes froze. I couldn't believe what I saw: a garish blue and orange building at least twenty storeys high. On the very top were aerials and antennae, the equivalent at least of another four storeys. It dominated the entire skyscape. Who on earth had sanctioned the construction of this monstrosity? This is Malta, not Manhattan.

Then it dawned on me. It was the giant communications mast that gave it away. Mobile phones and satellite communications! This was the 21st century equivalent of the Cable and Wireless Office and, come to think of it, it was built not too far from the old site. Oh well, I suppose it had to happen. Making enquiries later it seems that much thought had gone into its colour scheme with the blue blending with the sky and the pale orange with the weathered limestone so prevalent in local buildings. At least somebody had made the effort, it seems. Its correct name is the Portomaso Business Tower and it has an excellent bar called Club 22 on the twenty-second floor – but sshh, don't tell everybody. Needless to say the view is superb, particularly at night.

Breakfast over, and far too much fried bread having been consumed, we set off to walk into town. It was warm but not too hot. I was terribly impressed with the new (at least to me) Promenade which I was told stretched from St. Julians to Qui Si Sana, about three miles away, where you had to cross the road to reach Tigne Beach. We walked past the end of Dingli Street and followed the bend to the right. The Italianate building at the bottom of Dingli Street was now a branch of the Lombard Bank and I recalled the acronym for overpaid workers in the City of London – *Loads of money but a right dickhead.*

I kept my eyes skinned for the Meadowbank Hotel. It was no more. I couldn't spot Navarino Flats either where so many of Dad's Boys had lived and my school friend Heather Prince. They must have been tarted up and renamed. We kept heading towards town and I stared down at the well worn platforms of eroded limestone with aluminium ladders leading into the sea every so often, giving bathers access to the bluest sea in the world. It was time for a cooling drink and I approached a kiosk beneath a huge shading parasol. The girl on duty smiled in my direction.

'A Kinnie, please. I haven't had one for forty-five years.'

It tasted like nectar and I savoured every single drop without uttering a syllable. The lady declined payment. That's Malta for you.

'You weren't joking were you. Would you like another one?'

I politely declined. No other drink in the entire world tastes like Kinnie. It says on the bottle that it is made from bitter oranges and aromatic herbs. Think of bitter lemon then switch your brain to oranges. Then add oregano and rosemary and you've probably just about got it. I am convinced it could be a successful cult drink if properly marketed in the UK. Another advantage is that it is totally non-alcoholic although some locals like it with a nip of gin added.

I stuck to the railing side and looked down to the water's edge. The Chalet Ghar Id Dudd had gone, completely. All that was left was a wide ribbon of stone and concrete which had formed the original base. It stuck out into the sea like a giant headstone that had fallen over. Some workmen were on it shovelling concrete into cracks and holes in its surface, to what end I don't know. It seemed an exercise in futility to me. Later enquiries revealed it had fallen victim to a particularly severe storm many years earlier. Where would kids roller skate now? Maybe they don't and of course it's skateboards and roller blades now anyway isn't it? I felt like I had lost an old friend.

We took a bus into Valletta, my first Maltese bus ride in four decades. The fare was 47c in euros. It suddenly dawned on us that we had no coins. Thomas Cook's Bureau de Change don't give you coins. Terry proffered a five euro note and the grumbling driver gave him four euro coins. There was a large tin full of loose change and the driver chucked a few coins into it 'for the church' no doubt. Oh well. I swear they were the same buses that had been on the road in 1963.

I day dreamed all the way as we passed Marks & Spencer's on the right and Manoel Island boatyard on the left. Some of the vessels looked as if they had been there since 1963. Maybe they had. Most of them looked old enough. There weren't any warships though, British or American. We went past the little humped-back bridge that linked Manoel Island to the mainland (if you can call Malta mainland) and headed for Ta'Xbiex (Tash Beesh). I felt as if I had never been away until we rounded a sharp bend and there on the right was a brand new apartment block called Forth Apartments. It was obviously named after HMS *Forth*, a huge submarine depot ship which had anchored in Msida Creek for years. In its day the *Forth* had been a major surface unit of the Mediterranean Fleet and capable of acting as mother ship to nine submarines at the same time. It was furnished with eight four-and-a-half-inch guns. It finished its active life as a floating dormitory for hundreds of Queen Alexandra Nurses stationed on Malta in the fifties and sixties. I'll bet a lot of 'nooky' went on aboard her. Another vessel that had spent much of her later life in Msida Creek was the *Star of Malta* in which my grandparents had made the journey to Malta in 1953. She wasn't there now, though, as she had been sold for scrap and broken up in La Spezia, Italy, in 1966. We had seen her many times en route to Valletta for shopping trips.

We got off the bus at the Phoenicia Hotel in Floriana just outside the gates to Valletta, except that there were no gates. They had gone. The nuns had gone too. It was simply heaving with people walking in both directions to and from the City. It was around lunchtime by now and office girls zipped in and out of shops and cafés buying snacks and cooling drinks. There were tourists everywhere. You could hear their conversations as you walked past them. They seemed to speak every language under the sun German, French, Italian and others of Eastern European origin including Russian. I had been taken aback by the number of Russians in Cyprus a few years earlier and now they were here too. On my island! Bloody Ruskies. Why don't they holiday on the Black Sea instead?

It was past high noon, our self imposed ruling for the consumption of alcohol and we grabbed a couple of seats in the outdoor area of the Café Royale. It looked out directly over the ruins of the old Opera House which had been flattened by Italian and German bombers in 1942. The broken but still vertical Corinthian stone columns had been left as a reminder of less happy days. Two Hop Leafs arrived with a pleasant Maltese waitress; Terry lit the first of several roll-ups and we just sat and watched the world go by.

Across the road were the early signs that a major building and reconstruction project was in the offing. A giant, artist's impression afforded the viewer a glimpse into the future and of what lay in store. It was no less than a new Parliament Building in the shadow of the Opera House itself. The chief architect was to be none less than the famed Italian Renzo Piano. If you do need an architect you might as well get the best. I walked across the road and read the long explanation of what the project was all about then returned to my friend and a fresh, cool beer that the waitress had just delivered. She had watched me studying the billboard.

'It is awful, don't you think? Just terrible. Why don't they just leave it as it is I just don't know.'

But that, in my opinion, is one of the problems with Malta. They leave far too much as it is, including piles of rubble from 1942 bomb sites and piles of rubble from 2012 building sites.

It would be fair to say that the week's trip was a mixture of reminiscences for me and adventures for Terry. Sitting in the open air café at Luqa Airport and enjoying a last beer I looked out at the tarmac and saw planes from a half a dozen countries. The electronic departure board informed us of the airlines and their destinations. Emirates to Larnaca and Dubai. Alitalia to Rome. Air France to Paris Charles de Gaulle. Ryan Air to Leeds/Bradford. Air Malta to London Heathrow. Air Malta to Brussels and of course our flight, Thomson's to Manchester. I reflected on just how far my little island had come in forty years. All this commercial aviation was a far cry from a squadron of Canberra bombers and a daily BEA flight to Heathrow. This was progress, real international commerce, and a million light years away from being simply a military base of a declining Empire.

I was always proud of my birthplace but after this trip I was positively enthused by what I had seen. I resolved to return as soon as I could. Work on my first novel, *Your Country Needs You,* and other commitments delayed my next trip until almost a year later.

'Can I come, Boy?' asked Terry once more.

'Of course you can!'

We travelled with Air Malta this time on an almost new Airbus A320 from Manchester. The plane was full, mostly with British tourists, but I recognised the accents and a few words of Maltese from several passengers whom I suspect had been visiting friends and family in the North of England. For over a century there had been a great deal of intermarriage between Brits and Maltese, mostly between Servicemen and local Maltese girls. In fact one of Dad's old Boys from the early days at Dingli, one Ken Garnet, had married Nina, a Dingli village Beauty Queen. They had six children so just think how many of those Greek, Phoenician, Arab and Roman genes are being carried into the future by their children. Although widowed now and in her eighties, Nina was unmistakably Maltese in voice and gestures. She still made me the finest timpanas and in return I would bring her back copies of the *Times of Malta*. She pored over every word, I know she did.

Unfortunately this trip was affected by a short illness of Terry's. Shortness of breath on the plane was followed the next day by acute chest discomfort and the hotel doctor was called. He quickly prescribed some medication which unfortunately was not available at the nearest pharmacy so I took a taxi to Mater Dei, Malta's premier and showpiece hospital. The taxi driver said he would wait outside while I went to the pharmacy clutching the written prescription. I was only inside for ten minutes and the driver had barely finished a fag when I returned. The pharmacist who helped me gave additional advice for me to pass on to Terry, informed me that no financial transaction was necessary and bade me good day. I was back at the hotel within another twenty minutes and I gave the driver a healthy tip on top of the fare.

'That was quick, Boy. You were less than an hour.'

It was yet another reminder, as if one was needed, that Malta had come a long way. Forty years earlier it might have been the long trek to Bighi Hospital. The gleaming edifice that was Mater Dei Hospital was already internationally renowned for its excellence and a destination for medical tourists from all over Europe. It seemed to me like a 21st century continuance of the Knights Hospitallers of the 15th century, no less.

Terry's recovery was rapid. We decided to take in a trip to Ghajn Tuffieha. Out of the blue one day Terry mentioned that he had been stationed there when he was in the Marines and did I know where it was? Did I know where it was? I ask you!

I consulted the bus map to ascertain the correct bus (it was a 225) and we climbed aboard and paid the fares in cash. The 'seven day pass' had yet to be adopted let alone the infamous Tallijna which would become Malta's equivalent of London's oyster card. The bus didn't take the route I anticipated. After leaving St. Julians and going up the hill past Dick's Bar it turned west onto a new road that was unfamiliar to me. In fact this whole built up area was new to me. It simply didn't exist in 1963. Going uphill all the time we soon arrived into more open countryside and there were signs for Naxxar which I remembered well as the site of the trade fair and my first taste of rabbit with the Bezzina brothers, Charles and Walter. We went past the huge church and I spotted a fine new building on the left that had been built in the old style but with new stone. It looked like a miniature fort complete with a flagstaff. We soon passed through Mosta and the famous Dome.

My eyes searched for the main post office where Dad had to pay one shilling duty on the airmailed tin of Quality

Street in 1960. I couldn't see it. Maybe it has been moved to a more modern building. The road passed over the ditch known as the Wied ta Isperanza which in the winter had a small river flowing through it. However the vegetation looked lush in summer. Next stop was the small town of Mgarr which is also dominated by the huge Church Regina. I immediately recalled it from Dad's famous days of ecclesiastical photography. It was extremely photogenic, if indeed any inanimate object can be, and its relatively new limestone façade shone brilliantly in the hot sun. A mobile fruit and veg shop had parked very awkwardly near the sharp ninety degree bend and the owner and our driver exchanged rude greetings and epithets as we had to make several reversing manoeuvres before the bus negotiated the bend. Ten minutes later and we pulled into the little terminus at Ghajn Tuffieha, or Golden Bay, as tourists called it. Fifty yards away was the welcoming sight of the Apple's Eye café and bar. Two cold Hop Leafs please!

We took our beers out onto the large verandah and I looked behind Terry's shoulder, pointed and said: 'Well, there it is, mate. There's your Marines Camp.'

Even for me it took a while to sink in. Nothing had changed, simply nothing. There, about four hundred yards distant, was the whole Camp, exactly as I remembered it from 1963. There in front of my eyes was the Carr's residence, the Camp church, the NAAFI and all the other buildings. Terry's eyes were transfixed. He even spotted his old billet. I cannot tell you what was going through his head. He had last been here in 1956 when doing the final training before going to join the Suez campaign.

After two more beers we decided to go and take a closer look. Walking back past the bus stop we found large iron gates at the entrance to the open ground surrounding the Camp. There was a large notice that read *Keep out. Authorised Personnel Only.* But how old was the sign? You never knew in Malta. Was the order still current? It could conceivably have been there since the Marines left. A large metal bolt kept the two main gates clamped together but further inspection revealed that the attached padlock was not even locked. I slipped it off, slid the bolt and pushed gently on the gates. They opened only a short way so I leaned into them. The right hand side opened a good two feet.

'Come on, Boy, let's take a look.'

We walked slowly in the heat, the odd grasshopper jumping away from the dry tufts of grass and wild aniseed. On the right was what was left of the assault course that had given Brian and me so much pleasure. An artificial ship's mast looked much smaller and newer than the one I remembered. We walked, slightly uphill, as Terry slowly got his bearings. He swept his arms round in a semi-circle.

'All this area here, Boy, is where most of the lads were all under canvas. Dozens of tents, hundreds of blokes. Let's go as far as we can.'

We reached his old stone built billet. Outside it was a washroom and small toilet block.

'I don't believe it. Even the old shithouse is still here!'

That's Marines for you I guess. The opportunity to take a photo of Terry posing outside his old khazi was too good to miss. We didn't stay too long. It was very hot indeed and we retraced our steps back to the Apple's Eye. Two more Hop Leafs please. Cheers! Bis sahha tieghek! We got the same bus back half an hour later. We resolved to come back again on our next trip to Malta. This was just a short Monday to Friday hop and we wanted to venture forth to new territory in the remaining time.

The next morning we took the 222 to Cirkewwa where was situated the new ferry terminal to Gozo. It took an hour to complete the bus ride. It was like a long winding trip down memory lane for me. First I spotted Jessie's Bar where I had waited for the Army ambulance to take me to Bighi Hospital. Then, on the right, was St. Andrew's School which looked as if it had been in a time warp. Mr Ozouf may still have been sitting in his office reading my *Diary of Naples*. The bus trundled on past St. Andrew's and St. Patrick's Barracks, or what was left of them, and headed for Salina Bay and the salt pans.

On the edge of the pans, adjacent to a stagnant looking stream, were several large timber sheds used to store the collected salt. They were falling down in 1963 but here we were in 2009 and they were still falling down. The bus detoured round Buggiba, a horrid touristy area that didn't even exist in 1963, and headed into the village of St. Paul's Bay. We passed a large house on the right with a large front garden with palms growing in it. I recognised it immediately. An old classmate called Christopher la Nice had lived there with his parents. Chris's dad was a diplomat whose status demanded a house, not a flat. He was a nice guy, Chris, and I pinched his name for a character in my first novel, *Your Country Needs You*. Sir Michael de la Nice was the head of the Civil Service in my book and the only person who commanded Her Majesty's total confidence. I'm sure Chris would roar his head off if he ever read it.

Slowly but surely the bus headed north and a short time later the road rounded the bend at the head of the Bay and headed northeast up XemXija Hill. A hundred memories came flooding back. Dolphin Flats had been redeveloped and become Dolphin Court, no doubt at a proportionately higher rental. Our old potato patch was built on and there lots of shiny new blocks of flats, particularly on the left hand side of the road. The majestic view was of course still majestic. The bus carried on past the turn off to Mistra Bay and headed uphill to Melieha. We passed the beach which was crowded with sun bathers, swimmers and wind surfers. It was probably the safest beach for kids on the island as you could walk out into the sea for fifty yards and still be only knee deep. We passed the turn off for Paradise Bay and I smiled to myself as I wondered if SPURS was still displayed in concrete on the bottom step.

Then suddenly I saw it.

It was about half a mile west of the old terminal at Marfa. I was stunned. The terminal was massive and you would think that it was Dover or Calais with signs everywhere directing cars and passengers in this and that direction. This place could have handled the Dunkirk evacuation. I could see one ferry with its jaws-style bow doors open and two, yes two, cars waiting to drive up the ramp. We bought our tickets as foot passengers and made our way up escalators towards the departure area. The penny dropped. Of course. This was part of the largesse so prevalent and visual in the far flung outposts of the New Empire. The EU, the European Union, was at work. Fairly soon I saw it. A large plaque on the wall. *This Gozo Channel Terminal has been part funded by the European Union.* Alongside it was the ubiquitous blue flag with its twelve yellow stars in a circle so perfect in its precision that only a computer can draw it.

The ferry was huge for the two cars and maybe fifty passengers aboard. There was an excellent little café that sold coffee, beer and snacks and to my amazement a small bookshop. As with most bookshops in Malta, which seem to pop up in the most unlikely places, books with the flavour of Malta predominate. Immediately on view and by far the most prominent was *The Kappillan of Malta*, by Nicholas Monsarrat. I was not in the least surprised to see it on display. Monsarrat had actually written it whilst living on Gozo. I had read it myself twenty years earlier and I thought it was a better book than *The Cruel Sea* which had gained the author his greatest fame.. I bought a copy on the boat and presented it to Cathi Poole, my publishing editor in York. I never did ask her what she thought of it.

Twenty minutes and two beers later we berthed at the pretty harbour of Mgarr, Gozo's ferry terminal. There were more big glossy buildings, escalators and, of course, another EU plaque. I dare say that some non-elected, unaccountable, bloated and overpaid eurocrat had flown in from Brussels and cut a ribbon to officially open it. Let's hope he remembered to open the other terminal in Malta on the same day.

It was very hot and so we took a taxi into Rabat and had a mooch round. We found a grocer's that doubled up as a bar and bought two Hop Leafs for a euro each, the cheapest price we had ever paid. The owner brought us two stools and a small table and an ashtray for Terry. We watched the world go by. The pace of life was very slow and in stark contrast to the hum and buzz of Sliema. A lone policeman strode out of the police station diagonally opposite, took not the blindest bit of notice of the traffic lights and walked into the shop. After buying a beer, some water and a newspaper he strode back to the station, totally oblivious to anybody else, let alone the traffic.

Two cars were parked right on the corner with the drivers talking to each other through the car windows. The lights changed several times but the cars didn't move, the drivers still chatting. The shop owner brought us two more beers without being asked. I decided I liked this place. In fact

I liked it a lot. Feeling peckish I asked a passing girl called Gina for directions to a good café or whatever. Walking through a park and down a long hot road we ended up at Eldorado's. Despite its Spanish name it was every inch Maltese – or should I say Gozitan? Several large family groups were lunching there and, as they say, if the locals eat there it must be good. The timpana I ate certainly was. We got a bus back to Mgarr and took the ferry back to Malta. And so ended my first trip to Gozo since my last one with Mum, Dad and Norman Fox forty-six years earlier. Wow!

I recount these tales because I want to try and put some perspective into how I view Malta, and Gozo, today. It is not easy, believe me.

The next day we took a harbour cruise, buying tickets from a booth near to the Valletta Ferry terminal. The tall young man who sold me the tickets seemed a cheerful chappie and as the sailing time was still twenty minutes away I got into conversation with him. His name was Chris Galea and his unusual accent interested me. It had a distinct twang that you don't normally associate with Maltese speaking in English. He had, he explained, been born in Wollongong, New South Wales. His father had emigrated from Malta to Australia many years earlier and married an Aussie girl, his mother Susan. He and his brother Jean-Paul had both been born in Wollongong but, like a sardine swimming against the shoal, his father had turned his back on the Lucky Country and come home bringing his new family with him. It was yet another example of the links between the two countries, one a tiny island the other a giant island continent. From that day until now I always have a chat if I spot Chris on the waterfront.

The harbour cruise was pleasant although most of the sights were familiar to me including the old, now disused,

Bighi Hospital where I had my fractured arm set in plaster. One thing was new, though, a huge new drydock dubbed the Red Dock as it had been constructed in French Creek courtesy of the People's Republic of China. It was built after the dreadful split between the British and Maltese Governments which I will touch on later.

On the final day we took the bus to Marsaxlokk, a pretty fishing village in the extreme southeast of the island. The colourful and numerous fishing boats are the subject for thousands of postcards on sale at every souvenir shop on the island. We bought lace tablecloths to take back for wives and friends and some clover honey for my neighbour Barbara who looks after my house for me while I'm away in warmer climes. One of the vendors warned us that some imitation Chinese copies were creeping into the marketplace and that we should be careful. The *Made in Taiwan* engraving on a metal clip holding a dozen or so place mats together did not exactly instil confidence in any of her merchandise. Before catching the bus home we had beer, sandwiches and chips on the outside seating area of the Duncan Hotel. The friendly proprietor, Michael Baldacchino, had a clipped English accent. You didn't need to ask where he had spent half of his life: in his case it was Sydney, NSW.

Back in England by the weekend Terry reflected on how his old Camp could still be here but not be used for anything. Malta didn't need a Marine Corps, that's for sure, but surely such a huge area could be utilised for something. We decided to go back again the following year.

By then I was a devout fan of *Air Malta* and I booked the flights and hotel rooms separately. I just didn't fancy BudgetAir.com with long queues of half-cut human dross seeking instant sunburn and cheap booze. Call me a snob if you like. Flying *Air Malta* you feel as if you are there as soon as you step on the plane. That's where most airlines go wrong.

On boarding you are greeted by real people with real names like Carmen, Theresa and Marianne. Don't expect any Chloes, Shazzas or Bex. There aren't any. You are offered a courtesy copy of today's *Times of Malta* and if you are unfamiliar with the A320's seating plan you are shown to your seat. The cabin crew are immaculate. The Captain introduces him or herself to you, always by their full name. My first Air Malta Captain was called Denise but I cannot remember her surname. It reminded me of the time I flew from Melbourne to Tasmania on a QANTAS 737 and the Captain introduced herself as Captain Vic Johnson.

'G'day I'm Vic Johnson, that's Victoria by the way, your Captain today, but don't worry fellas I don't have to reverse it!'

I don't suppose that was taken from the flight manual but you know what Aussies are like. Air Malta's in-flight magazine is called *Il-Bizzilla* (The Malta Lace) and is the best, by far, I have seen anywhere in the world. There are no ads for perfumes, gadgets and other junk that you don't need. It whiles away at least an hour of the three hour flight and presents the visitor, particularly the first time visitor, with a taste of Malta's seven thousand year old history together with a hint of its 21st century present. I wish you could subscribe to it like a magazine and receive it through the post every month.

I would not class myself as an aviation anorak but I often do take notice of aircraft registration numbers which you cannot always see because of those metal tunnels you use to board planes these days. At Luqa, thank goodness, you board via steps in the time honoured way and this affords you the chance of a final look around at the sun, the sky and, if visible, the registration number. On no fewer than eight occasions I have flown on A319 9H-AEG. Intrigued, I went online to do a little research and discovered that the plane's name was M'dina. I thought that was most appropriate considering that M'Tarfa, where I was born, is only a stone's throw away.

On our next visit to Ghajn Tuffieha and the old Marines Camp there was a new sign on display. Those large iron gates were partly open and several cars were parked about a hundred metres (I've now gone metric) inside the grounds. The new sign announced that the area had been handed over to the Scout Movement. Progress indeed! We followed the direction we had taken almost a year earlier and were pleased to see some people looking around Terry's old billet. A pleasant chap, in his forties probably, was astonished to hear Terry's story of being based here for training in 1956. When I told him I used to play on the assault course with my friend Brian as a ten year old he was even more surprised. This gentleman was somehow involved with the Scouts and went on to tell us that progress was very slow in renovating the buildings which it was hoped in time would provide facilities for Scout camps at weekends and in school holidays. The problem, he explained, was a shortage of money to do the job. I recommended to him to apply for a grant from the EU as they appeared to have oodles of it.

Joking apart, this was very encouraging. There was still the problem of what the Malta Government intended to do with the other hundred odd hectares of land and buildings which also included a shooting range where decades earlier Brian and I used to find live rounds of ammo and loose change that had fallen out of pockets of Marines' fatigues as they lay prostrate on the ground aiming their Belgian rifles at cardboard cut-outs of the enemy a hundred yards away.

Britain always seemed to be fighting a War somewhere in the world whether it was in East Africa, the Gulf or South East Asia. Royal Marines were always in the vanguard and the thick of the action. *Per Mare Per Terram* (by sea by land) is their motto and they were surrounded by both here at Ghajn Tuffieha.

Progress has been painfully slow with the Scouts project but facilities are improving judging by the photograph of Terry set against the backdrop of his old billet. Would Captain Carr have approved of the bright blue shutters instead of dark green ones? Maybe Mrs Carr might. I am happy to tell you that Joan is still with us, in her nineties and living in Portsmouth. On my most recent visit I spoke to some Irish Scouts who had set up camp there. They looked pale and sunburnt at the same time. Hadn't anybody told them that in July Malta is hot and dry? There were still no fans in the billets let alone air conditioners. Innocents abroad if you ask me. They looked happy, though, which is what Scouting is all about.

On my next trip back to Malta, which was on my own, I decided to explore more of the old Sliema and Tigne that was such familiar territory all those years ago. Staying in the same hotel I followed the Promenade all the way to its very end turning into Qui-si-Sana. Some of the buildings were the original ones, others brand new. Hesitating, I turned into Hughes Hallet Street and strode uphill mindful of seeing ghosts from yesteryear. The hotel annex called *Cathay* had gone and been replaced by a fine looking block of apartments. They might have kept the name for sentiment's sake but they hadn't. On my left, on the corner was the old Plevna Hotel looking exactly as it had done forty-seven years earlier. I wondered who had watched the FA Cup final this year and whether the Tabona family still owned the hotel. It was looking as smart as ever. Suddenly there was a gap on my right that you could drive a coach and horses through. I took a look and found myself staring at the grounds of the old Union Club. It looked totally derelict, even worse than in 1963. How could a huge piece of valuable real estate still look like a waste tip? Then, suddenly, I was upon it. London Stores once known to us as Freddies. Boxes of oranges, lemons and melons were displayed on the pavement and in the window were bottles of olive oil and wine. My eyes quickly hunted for Ollio Sasso but I couldn't see it. Should I go in? Dare I go in?

I saw a person moving in the shop, probably a customer, so I joined him. It soon dawned on me it was the shopkeeper.

'Good morning, can I help you?'

This chap was eighty if a day. No it can't be... surely not.

'Good morning... you're not... you're not Freddie are you, Sir?'

'No, I am his brother Joseph. Who are you?'

So I told him the whole story. He remembered my father, mother, sister and myself very well. He told me that my father had visited him some years ago. Then I remembered that Dad and Ken Garnet had taken a trip there in 1993 the year after Mum died. I might even have a photo somewhere. I enquired about Freddie, half expecting to receive bad news.

'Freddie is fine thank you. Last year we decided to branch out and we opened another store in Msida.'

Can you believe that? Two brothers in their eighties opening a new store a couple of miles away. I promised to return, hopefully with a photograph next time. We shook hands. It was time for his siesta. At his age I didn't blame him.

I looked over the road at Mirabell House. It looked scruffy and run down and the balcony of our old flat was covered in plant pots and what looked from below like a fish tank. Entering the foyer I walked up all the stairs, past the door to number five and headed for the roof. The view over the Union Club towards the Promenade was the same – minus the Chalet Ghar Id Dudd of course. But worse was to come. A new block towered above Mirabell slap bang next door and the view of Manoel Island and Sliema Creek had gone for ever. I stayed there for several minutes collecting my thoughts. Maybe I shouldn't have gone back but I did and I'm glad I did.

I walked down Tigne Street past the Cosstick's block of flats which didn't seem to have altered at all and headed for the Gunners Rest. But it had gone! The shop was still there but it no longer sold the *Daily Express,* war comics and Airfix model aeroplanes. The entrance to the old Tigne Barracks where I used to catch the Army truck to Cubs was right ahead of me. I was absolutely astounded, there is no other word for it, with what I saw. The barracks had been demolished but much of the stone had been recovered, restored and used again to build the most magnificent replica of a colonial, colonnaded Army edifice that you could imagine. It is breathtaking.

But what had it become? I saw a sign to my left: *Sliema Wanderers F.C.* What, a football club? Where, for goodness sake? It was 'Members only' so I walked on past. The next door was much bigger and I saw a lady with several kids coming out so I walked in. Like a grotto opening up before my eyes was this unbelievable shopping mall. I had accidentally stumbled into Tigne Point, Malta's biggest mall. It was built on four levels, three of them underground, and all linked by escalators. It occurred to me that the civil engineers who had built this wonderland had taken advantage of the large underground magazine that I knew existed when it was used by the British Army. And all this was achieved without EU money. Oh yes, before I forget, Sliema Wanderers' football pitch is on the roof, utilising an artificial playing surface. If you don't believe me, look on Google Earth.

On another day I decided to go to St. Paul's Bay via Buggiba, a tourist area that didn't exist in 1963. After getting off the bus at the terminus I first decided to try and look up a lady Terry and I had met at Luqa Airport when leaving at the end of the last trip. Her name was Claudia Camilleri, a vivacious and attractive girl who at the time worked for Ambrosia Wines of Gozo. I was in luck and found her, by chance, at her parents' house. I suggested we went to St. Paul's Bay for lunch so we went in her car and parked near to what I call the St. Paul's Shipwreck Chapel.

I was hoping to catch sight of the Harbour Bar with its lobster pool but it had all been redeveloped. Claudia recommended that we lunch at the Gillieru Hotel and Restaurant, a fairly new development on the water's edge. After taking our orders I told the manager of my adventures as a small boy and how I would haul in a lobster and then throw it back in.

'When was it all redeveloped? And what happened to the pool?'

'Come with me. I will show you something.'

He led me downstairs and there under the new building was the old pool! The manager, Steve, gave me his business card which I still have today. No wonder it says: *Gillieru Restaurant. Specialising in Fresh Fish.* It made my day. Claudia's company was nice too and she kindly gave me a lift back to Sliema.

Three years ago, in 2012, I decided to look up the David Bruce Hospital which I knew had become a school – St.

Nicholas College. I telephoned in advance and made an appointment to meet a Doris Vincenti, an English teacher. She was charming and fascinated to hear I had been born there. I also met Mr Jude Zammit and together they showed me around the huge building which had not been used as a hospital for years. Little things though gave away bits of its history such as an electrical wall socket in Jude's office that had a sticker over it saying *X-ray only*. Many of the former hospital wards were simply empty. You would need hundreds of pupils to fill a school as big is this. In the entrance hall were pictures painted by some of the pupils. One of them was of the oil tanker *Ohio* entering Grand Harbour in 1942. My publishers and I would have liked to instigate a story writing competition for the school with prizes for the winners. Sadly, Government funding for Maltese schools was being reallocated and the future of St. Nicholas College was in some doubt so my idea, thus far at least, has not come to fruition. Maybe one day.

I had often wondered whence the former Naval and Military Hospital had derived its name. The answer, when it came, was a revelation. Doctor David Bruce was the son of Scottish parents who had emigrated to Australia and the man himself was born in Bendigo, Victoria. They returned to Scotland where David qualified as a doctor. Whilst working in Malta and attending to wounded troop he noticed a high prevalence of what he called Malta fever and he guessed, correctly, that it might be caused by drinking local goat's milk. Further research by others more qualified in bacteriology isolated the illness which then was given the name we know today as brucellosis. Perhaps that should be Brucellosis! So a hospital as well as an illness was named after David Bruce.

I mentioned at the outset that I have a likeness for gardening which I inherited from my grandad. Even that pastime has a Malta connection. Dad's eldest sister, Eva, did not manage to visit us when we actually lived on the island. However after she retired and sadly lost her husband Bill, who was himself a professional gardener with Greater London Council, she took a holiday to Malta staying at the Marina Hotel in Sliema front near the Ferries. She got hooked and not a year went by until she passed away without an annual visit, sometimes biannual. On one trip she decided to be very naughty and took a cutting from an oleander bush not far from the hotel. She brought it back in a polythene bag in her handbag and gave it to my father. He stuck some rooting powder on it and nurtured it. Twenty-five years later Eva the Oleander has flourished and as I write she is in full bloom in a huge pot on my patio. The changing of the clocks from British Summer Time to GMT is my cue to pop her into the greenhouse for the winter.

I am a very enthusiastic wine drinker: I'm not an expert or a connoisseur, I just like it. Long since gone are the days when Malta produced just a red, a white and a rosé. I sample as many different labels and wineries as my wallet and liver will allow. They are superb in taste and quality and offer excellent value for money. Many of the wineries are on Gozo and if I had to single out one to demonstrate Malta's excellence in the industry it would be the St. Jean Syrah from the Bacchus vineyard. I gave my last bottle to one Howard Hunter, a prominent member of the Yorkshire Guild of Sommeliers. Guess what? Within days of drinking it he organised a Club tasting tour to Malta and Gozo.

Earlier I mentioned postcards of Marsaxlokk with its pretty fishing boats. In fact most postcards on offer in a multitude of outlets are inexpensive and of a high quality.

I have always sent postcards home to friends and family – so much more personal and friendly that a banal and meaningless text or email. I like people to *see* where I am. To make it easier I can tell you that Malta Post is absolutely first class in every respect. OK, it's only a small island but when I tell you that cards I post to England on a Monday morning are delivered on Wednesday or Thursday at the very latest then you have to be impressed. That means that when taken from the traditional little red box in Sliema or wherever they are on a plane to London that same afternoon, are at Mount Pleasant sorting office in London the next morning and in Yorkshire or wherever the next day. Purely as an exercise I posted a card to myself from Sliema at lunchtime on a Thursday. I arrived home in Scarborough on the Saturday evening and the card was on the mat. Beat that! Malta Post, you are brilliant. Just one small point though, if I may. Why is the 'G.C.' no longer depicted on your colourful stamps?

I am glad I was not in Malta during the difficult years when our Governments fell out. Listening from afar to the squabbling about military bases and money was very upsetting. It was only right that Malta assumed Independence and true nationhood in 1964 but to fail to reach agreement over the paltry sum of a couple of million quid was just appalling. Today that same amount of wonga wouldn't even buy you a spare engine for a Typhoon, the Spitfire of the 21st century. The majority of the blame, in my opinion, must go to the autocratic and intransigent nature of senior British politicians. But who am I? I was only born in Malta and I'm not its Foreign Secretary, let alone its First Minister. Chance would be a fine thing. I wouldn't let anybody bully Malta.

I read the *Times of Malta* online nearly every day. Can somebody explain to me please why Air Malta is in financial trouble and is laying off planes in the winter? The population of Yorkshire is over five million, that's more than ten times Malta's. In winter we freeze our nuts off. Instead of mothballing your planes you should be flying round the clock to Leeds Bradford and Doncaster Robin Hood Airports. Get real and get here, Air Malta. I will pay a premium to take the inaugural flight from Doncaster.

But back to the future, as they say. Where does Malta go from here as a nation? I have heard it said that it might be the 'next Dubai'! Goodness me, I certainly hope not. Why would any nation, let alone one with an unbelievable and unique seven thousand year history, want to emulate one built on sand dunes from the fast falling revenues of a fossil fuel with a lifespan of several moths? If you want to look to a nation that has prospered from the skills of its people, enterprise and hard work then the example set by Singapore is a better model. Like Malta it is small, densely populated and was a former Crown Colony. From a trading point of view it is at the crossroads of Asia. Likewise, Malta is at the crossroads of the Mediterranean. They both have excellent aviation and shipping facilities. And they are both members of the Commonwealth as Republics. Adopting Singapore's litter laws might also be a good idea too, come to think of it.

Joining the EU Club, as it were, in 2004, might have seemed at the time to be the right thing to do with embracing the Euro four years later an almost automatic consequence. There is no doubt it was inflationary which is not good for tourism, Malta's main industry and revenue earner. Was it a wise move? Only time will tell but the omens, sadly, are not good. Look at Greece today. It is the world's oldest democracy and it is falling apart. I predict that much of the Eurozone will follow.

What will happen then to all those plaques reading *Partially funded by the European Union*?

When the EU folds up maybe they will be replaced by signs that read *Funded entirely by the Blood, Sweat and Tears of the People of the George Cross Island.* Now that would be worth celebrating. With a La Vallette, classic red of course.

In 2008 the effects of watching the *Flying Doctor* and *Ten Town* finally took hold and I flew to Perth, the State Capital of Western Australia, to see old friends and long lost cousins. Another reason for going there was to do a little research for *Her Place in the Sun*, the sequel to *Your Country Needs You*, set in Australia Whilst there I pondered on the idea of possibly buying a plot of building land as an investment. The smart young salesman who showed me round an area called Dog Swamp (honestly) gave me his business card before we parted company. His name was Paul Azzopardi. I gave it a double take.

'Your family is originally from Malta then, Paul.'

'Yih. Grandad came from a place called... er... Rabbit... or something like that anyway.'

'I think you mean Rabat, near to the old capital of M'dina.'

'Dunno, mate. He's no longer with us. No worries.'

And that was the end of the conversation. Later, over a few cold Swan Lagers, I pondered over whether his forebears had lived in a cave and reared turkeys. You just never know. And if they did then he was the poorer for not knowing.

After a couple of weeks in Perth (where they probably have the world's worst postal service) I flew two thousand miles east to Brisbane, Queensland. Strolling along the banks of the Brisbane River I noticed the Queensland State Flag fluttering atop the Parliament building. Set against a brilliant blue background was a Maltese Cross. I felt quite at home. Seemingly the Cross replaced the head of Queen Victoria when she died in 1901. But who made that decision and why? Answers on a postcard but post it from Malta, not Perth.

I decided to spend New Year 2015 in Valletta as a contrast to a summer holiday in Sliema. Big mistake: it was freezing, even to me. It actually snowed for a few seconds for the first time in over a hundred years. It was just bad luck.

My hotel on this occasion, the Osborne in South Street, had arranged for a chauffeur driven car to meet me at Luqa. Just as on that QANTAS flight to Hobart my Captain was a lady in the shape of the charming Josette Gauci. I'll tell you now, Victoria and Josette can fly and drive me anywhere they like any time. Staying in Valletta offered me the chance to see it at close quarters for the first time in fifty years. It was cool and the skies were mostly grey but you would have to be a Philistine not to appreciate the architectural magnificence of the city named after Jean Parisot de Valette, the 49th Grand Master of the Order of Malta. He commanded the resistance against the Turks and the Ottoman Empire in the Great Siege of Malta in 1565 which many military historians claim was the greatest defence of any nation in history.

I have two overriding memories of that cold New Year's Day. Walking down Republic Street, formerly Kingsway, a priest stood outside his church as the bells tolled way above our heads. He shook hands with every single person who passed by on the street and wished them a Happy New Year. How many places in the world would you see that? Minutes later I walked past St. John's Co-Cathedral. A busker had set up on the steps and he was playing an oboe linked by a microphone to a small portable speaker. The tune he was playing, appropriately, was *Gabriel's Oboe,* often called by its proper name *Nella Fantasia.*

He had barely played beyond the opening bars when a young girl, probably in her early teens, appeared from the gaggle of passers by, sat on the steps beside him and promptly started singing the lyrics to the tune in Italian. It was used as the theme tune to the movie *The Mission*. The oboist and the girl simply brought the house down. Three days later Josette drove me back to Luqa and my own personal Air Malta Airbus. Thank you, Valletta, I will stay with you again but preferably in warmer months.

Valletta is simply an amazing city and is destined to be European City of Culture in 2018. I never tire of watching the Noon Day Gun being fired from the Upper Barrakka Gardens. It is usually busy with tourists around that time and the view of the Three Cities and Fort St. Angelo is just awesome.

I celebrated my 60th birthday with friends in Malta and for several of them it was their first visit. Not so for Mike Davis who fifty-three years after we met at St. Andrew's School presented me that evening with a silver hip flask engraved *Happy 60th Mark. Mike & Julie. Malta G.C. 2013*. Wow!

We took the harbour cruise on the day itself and one of the girls said:

'I had no idea the harbour was this big, no idea at all.'

'Pauline, that's why it's called Grand Harbour!'

On another day on the same cruise I was lucky enough to see what is possibly the world's most expensive and beautiful yacht and I do mean yacht, not a souped up billion dollar oligarch's toy. If you have never seen the *Maltese Falcon* berthed alongside its spiritual home at Fort St. Angelo you are missing a treat. Named after the Humphrey Bogart movie it is eighty-eight metres of nautical majesty. I would love to just board her, let alone sail on her. How ironic though that she was built in modern Turkey which five hundred years ago, as the Ottoman Empire under the command of Suleiman the Magnificent, tried (and failed) to wrest Grand Harbour from the Noble Order of Knights.

And speaking of movies, Malta is now firmly established as a destination for a number of film producers. *The Mackintosh Man* made in 1973 starring Paul Newman and James Mason had the ending filmed in Valletta. It has been shown on TV in the UK several times as a good example of a Cold War thriller. *Popeye,* made in 1981, starring the late and much loved Robin Williams as the sailor himself, was filmed entirely in Malta; the purpose-built Popeye Village in Anchor Bay, north of Ghajn Tuffieha, is now a tourist attraction. Today, much of the spectacular *Game of Thrones* series is filmed in Gozo. I think it is certainly an industry that could thrive in Malta. Maybe I should write the script for a *Bond* movie set in Malta. Why not? *James Bond G.C.* Or how about *In the Bonds of the Order*? Now there's a thought!

I have a feeling in my waters that Malta's greatest days are yet to come. The hosting of the Malta Summit in 1989 was, I believe, a foretaste of a role that this island nation could fulfil in the centuries ahead. Whatever happens, Malta will need statesmen and women who believe in its future as well as admire its glorious past.

These then are my memories of Malta as a child and my experiences and thoughts thus far, half a century later, of Malta today and tomorrow. The Commonwealth Heads of Government Meeting in Valletta in November 2015 provided a timely reminder that unlike the inward looking EU the Commonwealth of nations is worldwide. Malta has more friends in that organisation than you could imagine and one day she might need them.

I must close now but before I do I want to assure you of one thing. My loyalty to the island that gave me my birth and infant nurture will never fade. I never did buy that plot of land in Australia. Perhaps I should look closer to home. Now let's see, Madliena looks quite nice …

Nigi lura Malta!

# PART 3

This section will, I hope, give you a few hints and ideas of how to get to Malta and, just as importantly, how to get around the island once you arrive.

If this is going to be your first visit to the George Cross Island then if you are a Brit you can relax – the locals nearly all speak English. For visiting Aussies, and there are thousands every year, many locals also speak Strine too! Such are the links between Malta and Australia.

As a two-year-old I flew from Malta to England (so I'm told) in a twin-engined Vickers Viking. Five years later as a very aware and curious seven-year-old I returned to Malta in a four-engined Vickers Viscount. I guess that was progress but both journeys still necessitated a re-fuelling stop in the south of France, the twelve hundred nautical mile sector proving too long for both aircraft types. In theory the Viscount could make it but not without adequate reserves and a headwind could cause a nasty stop in the oggin! The Mediterranean is not the Hudson River in New York.

Thankfully aviation has come a long way and today you can fly from one of many civil airports in the UK, non-stop, to Malta's International Airport. The ubiquitous Airbus A320 and Boeing 737 will provide the vast majority of flights and are quite comfortable for your journeys of usually no more than three and a quarter hours – slightly longer from Newcastle, Edinburgh, Glasgow and Belfast for obvious reasons.

The time difference between anywhere in the UK and Malta is always only one hour whether the UK is on either GMT or BST and your tickets and/or booking confirmation will always show the local times for departure and arrivals. Do not be hoodwinked into thinking that a benevolent tailwind will bring you home an hour quicker! If only.

Long since gone are days when BEA had a virtual monopoly of the UK to Malta route. Today you can go onto skyscanner.com and take your pick from a variety of airlines and routes. So wherever you live in the UK you can find an airline and an airport that is convenient for YOU. Living as I do in Yorkshire my default choice is to fly from Leeds Bradford Airport from where I can often find myself with a choice of two or even three airlines.

To my knowledge only Air Malta offers Club or Business Class so if you require extra space or comfort then you must consult the airline to see which seats offer extra leg-room. These are often located in the rows designated for emergency exits but these can vary between different marques of the same aircraft types so be warned. Check before you 'click and book' online.

You can however rest assured that your flight will be non-stop barring diversions for bad weather or other unforeseen reasons. For aviation buffs amongst you the main runway orientation is 13/31 which means its orientation is roughly NW/SE. If you are lucky your approach and descent into Malta will be from the North West on runway one-three, particularly if you arrive in daylight. Your final approach will be over Malta's sister island Gozo and then you descend over Mellieha and St. Paul's Bay. If seated on the port (left hand) side of the plane you will catch a magnificent glimpse of the iconic Mosta dome, the third largest in Christendom. Seconds after that you will be on the ground.

'Merhba t'Malta. Welcome to Malta!'

If you have booked a package which includes airport transfers to your hotel then on clearing Customs and Immigration keep your eyes skinned for a 'rep' from your travel company. He or she will be holding up a placard, perhaps saying 'Mercury' or 'Chevron' or if you are just a small party or travelling solo it might just display your surname 'Mr Bloggs.' Once you have been introduced to your rep then it is usually only a short walk on the concourse to your minibus or chauffeured car.

On the other hand if you have booked your flights independently and need to travel to your hotel then I recommend you take a white licensed taxi. There is a prominent taxi-booking booth by the main exit. Tell the clerk which hotel you want to go to and the lady will quote a fixed price. You pay in cash (Euros) and you will be handed a voucher which you give to the driver of the nearest taxi outside. The price is usually around twenty Euros. If you are tired after your flight this is the best way, trust me. It's true that there are designated Airport buses but unless you know the routes, times and your precise destination I would avoid them, at least on your first visit.

As in most parts of the world taxi drivers are a mine of information – and gossip! By the time you reach your destination it is likely that you will know where the driver lives, the names of his wife and kids, which Premiership football team he supports and how many relatives he has in England or Australia – or both! Tipping is practised and a couple of Euros 'for a beer' is always well received after the driver has placed your suitcases into the hotel lobby. Some will hand you their own business card and ask you to call them if you need a taxi during your visit. These guys are usually genuine and just looking to top-up their income a tad. This can be very useful when you make your return journey to the airport at the end of your holiday, assuming that you haven't booked a package tour. I have done this several times. Cheers, Mario!

If you are planning your *first* trip to Malta, perhaps on a recommendation from a friend, then you have *two* very important decisions to make. Firstly exactly *where* in Malta you wish to stay and secondly *when* to travel. Both these crucial decisions can make or break it for you.

Let's deal with the *where* first. Malta is not a big island – it's about half as big again as Jersey if you have been there. It measures approximately sixteen miles by ten but its coastline is very irregular with many bays and inlets including of course the famous Grand Harbour, one of the world's most perfect maritime havens. I recommend that you buy an *Insight Flexi Map* of Malta for around a fiver from *WH Smiths* or online. It is laminated (and thus waterproof) and easy to fold. Remember to take it to Malta with you!

What kind of holiday do you want? How physically mobile are you? What are your special interests, if any? All these factors have to be taken into consideration. If you're a young family with kids who want a beach, pool and sunshine holiday then you will be well catered for by a plethora of hotels and beach resorts in the Mellieha, Buggiba and Qawra areas in the north of the island. If night-life is your scene then the Paceville and Sliema areas will definitely float your boat. The history buffs amongst you would be advised to try the capital Valletta although hotels in this amazing city tend to be more expensive.

Malta has, as you might expect, a Mediterranean climate. This is true both geographically and meteorologically. Winters are mild, at least by UK standards, and summers are very hot. If you cannot deal with high temperatures and a fierce sun then you must avoid June to September. You will boil. If you're looking for warm and sunny days with temperatures around the twenty Celsius mark then Spring and Autumn are just perfect for you. Having said that you can get prolonged spells of warm and sunny weather in Malta's winter too but winter storms can be quite spectacular. It was one such storm that brought about St. Paul's shipwrecking and the arrival of Christianity to Malta.

So where does that leave you as you mull over a brochure or two or surf the internet on a wet and chilly Wednesday afternoon in Blighty? If you are retired and the actual timing of your first trip is up to you and not your workplace holiday rota, then I would say choose March/April or October/November for your first visit. The resort and venue is of course your choice and a multitude of websites and hotels will tempt you with deals. The north of the island, although more scenic, is quite hilly so if walking is your thing be warned. The resorts to the south like Marsascala and Marsaxlokk are relatively flat and offer fishing village type atmospheres. A downside though is that public transport to these areas can be slow and tedious. If you want a taste of everything that is Malta then a hotel in Sliema will offer you sea, restaurants and night-life with good bus connections to almost everywhere.

Which brings me nicely to transport and getting around. There are no trains or subway on Malta. There was a train that ran from Valletta to Rabat and M'Tarfa a hundred years ago, primarily to convey battle casualties to a military hospital. Sadly it closed decades ago which is a great shame.

If it was still operative today then it would be a major tourist attraction. So you are left with either buses or private cars. Although driving is on the left in Malta (as in the UK and Australia) my recommendation would be to stick to the buses, at least for your first trip, to get your bearings. There are far too many cars in Malta and it seems to be that every male driver under fifty has the genes of Ayrton Senna in his double helix.

The former colourful buses from the makers like Bedford and Plaxtons have mostly disappeared but their modern replacements are clean, air-conditioned and very efficient. The network extends to almost the whole of the island so wherever you want to visit is within reach. Some journeys will necessitate taking two buses with a change at Valletta along the lines of the "hub and spoke" principle. Your hotel will give you a free map of the bus routes which are colour-coded and easy to follow. If you have to change buses at Valletta then an electronic information board will give you a bus number, the bay number it will depart from and the time of departure. One thing I have learnt is that you must allow plenty of time for your journey. If you are travelling from say Sliema to Marsaxlokk for a mooch around and lunch at one of the many seafood cafes then allow a whole day for your excursion. You will enjoy it all the more at a leisurely pace anyway.

This is not intended to be a complete tourist guide. Places of interest abound, particularly if history is your chosen subject – Malta has over seven thousand years of it and some of its sites pre-date the Egyptian pyramids. Can you believe that? Buy a Berlitz or Dorling Kindersley guide for more details if you want to overdose on places of interest.

For the foodies amongst you I can advise that Malta's seafood is excellent and its wines are a revelation. You can trust me on that one, and I always take a bottle or two home with me which I buy at the airport. There are scores of eateries to choose from. Just leave that to Google or ask the staff in your hotel. The locals always know the best places!

Have fun and enjoy your first visit to '*My Island.*' I'm willing to bet that, for many of you, it will be the first of many.

For more information check out these websites

www.mvhbooks.com

www.seniorsonmalta.com